HAL LEONARD
GUITAR METHOD

JAZZ GUITAR

BY JEFF SCHROEDL

RECORDING CREDITS

Jeff Schroedl (Guitar), Mark Solveson (Bass), Ben Hans (Drums), Scott Currier (Piano), John Hibler (Sax)

PHOTO CREDITS

Frank Driggs Collection: 2 (Green, Christian, Kessel), 3 (Farlow, Green), 5 (Smith, Burrell)
Star File: 3 (Metheny), Robb Lawrence: 6 (left) courtesy of Wolf Marshall

ISBN 0-634-00144-2

HAL•LEONARD®
CORPORATION
7777 W. BLUEMOUND RD. P.O. BOX 13819 MILWAUKEE, WI 53213

Visit Hal Leonard Online at
www.halleonard.com

THE BASICS

WHAT IS JAZZ?

The American music known as "jazz" is nearly impossible to precisely define. Some players cite improvisation, others emphasize swing, while many contend that jazz's harmonic structures best characterize the style. In the dictionary, jazz is defined as: "A style of music of Afro-American roots characterized by a strong rhythmic understructure, 'blue' notes, and improvisation on melody and chord structure."

Although barely a century old, jazz has fostered many subcategories, including:

- *Dixieland*—New Orleans and Chicago small-band jazz style developed in the early 1900s, characterized by group improvisation over a steady two-beat ragtime rhythm. Notable proponents include King Oliver, Louis Armstrong, Jelly Roll Morton, and Sidney Bechet.

- *Swing*—big band music of the 1930s, characterized by a long-short, eighth-note (♫ = ♩♪) rhythmic feel. Notable proponents include the bands of Count Basie (Freddie Green, guitarist), Duke Ellington, Glenn Miller, and Benny Goodman.

- *Bebop*—a form of jazz originating in the 1940s, characterized by solo improvisations, complex rhythms, and extended harmonies. Notable proponents include Charlie Parker, Dizzy Gillespie, Thelonious Monk, and Bud Powell.

- *Cool Jazz*—a form of jazz originating in the 1950s, characterized by its subdued, ethereal approach, and experimental arrangements. Notable proponents include Miles Davis, Lennie Tristano, Gerry Mulligan, and Bill Evans.

- *Hard Bop*—derivatives of bebop in the mid-to-late 1960s, characterized by relentless rhythms (often bluesy or funky), extended solos, and enhanced accompaniment roles. Notable proponents include Horace Silver, Cannonball Adderley, Jimmy Smith, Grant Green, and John Coltrane.

- *Free Jazz*—a form of jazz originating in the 1960s, characterized by the lack of preset chords, melody, and form, as well as by complex and often chaotic improvisations. Notable proponents include Ornette Coleman, Cecil Taylor, Albert Ayler, and, to a certain degree, John Coltrane.

- *Latin Jazz*—a form of jazz initiated as musicians from Cuba, Puerto Rico, and South America incorporated an even-eighth note feel to the existing sensibilities of American jazz. "Latin" has since become a generic term, usually meaning a derivative of bossa nova or samba, both styles from Brazil. Notable proponents include Antonio Carlos Jobim, João Gilberto, Stan Getz, and Tito Puente.

- *Fusion*—a combination of jazz and rock dating from the late 1960s, characterized by inventive solos, rock-like rhythms and arrangements, and high volume, electric sounds. Notable proponents include Miles Davis, Chick Corea, John McLaughlin, the Brecker Brothers, and Pat Metheny.

Freddie Green, 1938

Charlie Christian, 1940

Barney Kessel, 1944

2

WHO'S WHO IN JAZZ GUITAR?

Listening is almost as much a part of learning to play jazz as practicing. In fact, much of the style's sum and substance is derived from oral tradition—handed down from player to player, recording to recording. Simply put, if you want to play jazz well, a combination of practicing, playing, *and* listening is essential.

More and more classic jazz guitar recordings are being reissued on CD each year. Of those released so far, here are fifteen milestone guitar recordings—in alphabetical order—that are strongly recommended:

1. George Benson—*Blue Benson* (Polydor)
2. Kenny Burrell—*Midnight Blue* (Blue Note)
3. Charlie Christian—*Solo Flight* (Stash)
4. Tal Farlow—*Tal* (Polygram)
5. Grant Green—*Matador* (Blue Note)
6. Jim Hall—*Jim Hall & Ron Carter: Alone Together* (Milestone)
7. Barney Kessel—*Poll Winners Three!* (Fantasy)
8. Pat Martino—*East!* (Prestige)
9. Pat Metheny—*Question and Answer* (Geffen)
10. Wes Montgomery—*The Incredible Jazz Guitar* (Riverside)
11. Joe Pass—*Joe Pass & Niels-Henning Ørsted-Pederson: Chops* (Pablo)
12. Jimmy Raney—*A* (Fantasy)
13. Django Reinhardt—*Djangology 49* (Bluebird)
14. Johnny Smith—*Moonlight in Vermont* (Roost)
15. Mike Stern—*Standards (and other songs)* (Atlantic Jazz)

Other players you should hear include George Barnes, Billy Bauer, Lenny Breau, Jimmy Bruno, Charlie Byrd, Larry Coryell, Herb Ellis, Bill Frisell, Mundell Lowe, John McLaughlin, Howard Roberts, John Scofield, Martin Taylor, George Van Epps, Mark Whitfield, and Jack Wilkins. Of course, there are many other wonderful jazz guitar players—past and present. For a complete listing of must-know jazz guitarists, including biographies and discographies, check out *The Jazz Guitar: Its Evolution and Its Players,* also available from Hal Leonard Corporation.

Listen to jazz played on other instruments, as well. A lot can be adapted from saxophone, trumpet, piano, and other prominent jazz instruments.

Tal Farlow, circa 1954

Grant Green, circa 1972

Pat Metheny, 1981

JAZZ PERFORMANCE ESSENTIALS

In jazz, it's very common for a group of strangers to get together to play, totally unrehearsed, on a gig in front of a live audience. As a result, there are certain terms and procedures that exist to ensure that things run smoothly.

Generally speaking, jazz songs follow a standard format: head in, solos, and head out. The term "head" refers to a tune's melody, which is played by one or more of the band's lead instruments while the rest of the band accompanies. Protocol says that once the head is played once or twice at the beginning of the piece, various soloists then improvise a solo based on the chord progression (or "changes") of the original melody. When the soloists are finished, the head is once again played and the song is ended.

Many songs also include intros, endings, and "trading" sections. Intros may be derived from a portion of the tune's form (often the last eight bars), a pedal on the fifth of the key, a spontaneous opening cadenza, or a specially composed part that takes the band into the head. There are several ways to end a song. Sometimes tunes have specific coda sections that provide an ending, oftentimes the last four or eight bars can be tagged or repeated to set up the end, occasionally a standard ritard (gradually slowing down) works, or players frequently will employ one of three or four cliché riff endings. Sometimes, usually right before the head out, musicians trade "fours" or "eights." This means that one soloist improvises over the first four (or eight) bars of the form, then another soloist improvises over the next four, and so on. There are a number of different ways to mix the trading up—probably the most common is to give the drummer every other four bars. Note that trading sections cover a tune's entire form, and should lead right back to the head, or top of the tune.

Structurally, most jazz tunes extend either 12, 16, 24, or 32 bars. It is important to recognize, and eventually memorize, the structure and form of the tunes you play. Musicians often refer to the first part of the form as the "A" section, and the second part as the "B" section, the bridge, the middle section, or the channel. Get used to keeping track of the form at all times—it is extremely important to maintain where you are at any given time in the tune.

You'll encounter many other survival situations in almost every gig you play. No book can truly prepare you for each and every encounter, but here are three things to watch out for: 1) Be aware of who might want to solo next; 2) If you're performing with a singer, be conscious of the key and entrance habits he or she prefers; 3) Mix up the tempos from song to song.

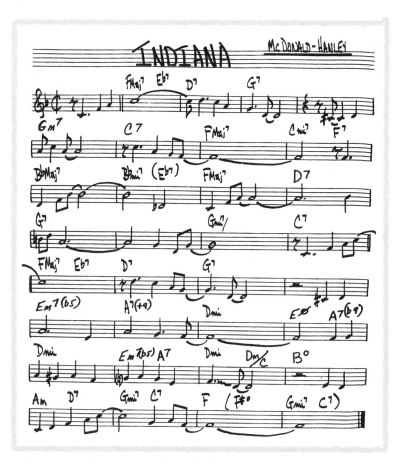

Most jazz combos read from a "lead sheet" similar to the one shown above. A
lead sheet provides the melody or "head," the changes, and the form of the tune.

THE GUITARIST'S ROLE

The instrumentation and setting of a jazz performance—whether you're gigging in a duo, trio, quartet, with or without a piano player, with or without a horn player, or with or without a vocalist—greatly dictates what the role of the guitar should be. Here are some things you should consider.

If you're playing in a conventional trio—guitar, acoustic bass, drums—first note that it's your duty to supply the harmony, or chords. (The following information also applies when playing duo with a bassist.) This can be done in two ways: by playing the head and improvising chord-melody style, or by intermittently placing chords within single-note phrases. Another option that exists is to play octaves. This doesn't provide chordal harmony, but it does help to fatten the group's overall sound. In reality, you'll probably want to mix all three ideas—starting sparse and building as the song progresses. For example, you might play the head the first time in a lower octave while throwing in very few chords. The second time through the head, you could move the melody up an octave, and add a few more chords. Next, begin your solo using only single notes. Then, still in your solo, transition to octaves and then to chord-melody style. And finally, after the bass and/or drum solos, take the head out by using a mixture of chord-melody, octaves, and single notes with chords.

When playing with a piano player, you need to adjust the above-mentioned approach quite a bit. In particular, when a guitarist and pianist are in the same ensemble, the pianist—due to their capacity to provide richer and thicker voicings—usually provides the majority of the harmony. However, keep in mind that sometimes the guitarist and pianist swap the comping duties. Also note that both the guitar and the piano are lead instruments—each capable of playing the song's melody. To avoid getting in each other's way during solos, most guitarists will employ single-note phrases, and in fact each instrument may drop out altogether during the other's solos.

In a setting that includes a horn player (sax, trumpet, etc.), usually the horn player will take the head. In this case, the role of the guitar is to play chords, and to solo when the time comes. If a piano player is already playing the chords, guitarists will sometimes double the head with the horn player, or lay out until it's their turn to solo. Note that on occasion, guitarists and pianists will both play chords at the same time, each being careful to avoid playing altered voicings that might clash with the other.

Playing with a singer requires an added responsibility for guitarists. Here, make sure you know a few intros that clearly set up the songs, and whenever possible, use chord voicings that contain the melody on top. Also, make sure you listen closely to how the singer approaches the end of the song—whether they're leading toward a tag, ritard, etc.—so you can make the changes necessary to ensure a smooth closing. (If the group includes a piano player, refer to the previous two paragraphs above regarding the usual guitar/piano protocol.)

On "society" and big-band swing gigs, the guitarist's role is usually to provide four-to-the-bar, Freddie Green-style comping. This means that the guitarist would play steady, quarter-note downstrums using simple three-note chord voicings located on the lower strings. Solos in this format are usually limited to the brass instruments, but occasionally guitarists are asked to play a role in this area.

The point is, it's important to prepare yourself for all types of settings. So as you listen, watch, and practice jazz, take note of how the various instruments interact within their respective ensembles.

Johnny Smith jamming in a trio with Artie Baker (clarinet)
and Lennie Tristano (piano), 1949

Kenny Burrell comps a C7 chord with the
Benny Goodman big band in 1957

EQUIPMENT AND SOUND

The sound of jazz guitar is much different than that of rock and even blues—and not only because of the notes, chords, and compositions. The equipment, too, plays an important role in the overall tone and timbre. Guitarists should keep in mind the type of guitar, amp, and gauge of strings.

Most jazz players prefer a "mids-heavy" clean tone using the neck pickup with the tone knob backed off slightly. This is a broad generalization, but for the most part, traditional jazz guitarists favor a relatively dull, round sound.

Heavy-gauge strings are the standard among most jazz guitarists—the typical .009s used by most rock players will sound too thin. Instead, most jazzers prefer either .012-.052 or .013-.056 sets.

The ideal choice of guitar varies. Through the years, players have adopted a plethora of brands and body styles that function well within the jazz idiom:

- The single-cutaway, electric archtop hollowbody—like the Gibson L-5 or ES-175—has always been one of the most popular jazz guitars for its fast, smooth action and rich tone. Wes Montgomery's use of it encouraged many others, like Joe Pass, Herb Ellis, and Pat Metheny. Today, these bigger body semi-acoustic electrics are made by many manufacturers, including Gibson, Benedetto, D'Aquisto, and Guild, among many others. The list of endorsees includes Jim Hall, Mark Whitfield, Jimmy Bruno, and Jack Wilkins, among others.

- If you are going for a slightly less traditional, more jazz-rock tone, you will find it much more easily obtainable from a thin body, semi-acoustic guitar—like the Gibson ES-335. Players such as Larry Carlton, Robben Ford, Lee Ritenour, and John Scofield have often sought this type of body style for its sustain, warmth, and overall versatility.

- And don't count out the solidbody guitar. Mike Stern, Pat Martino, and John Abercrombie all manage to get a terrific sound out their respective axes. So instruments like the Gibson Les Paul, Yamaha Pacific, and Parker Fly are also suitable for jazz.

As for amplifiers, once again there are many popular choices. In terms of tube amps, the elite would have to include the Fender Twin Reverb, Ampeg Reverb-o-Rocket, and Fender Tweed Pro. Meanwhile, Mesa-Boogie tube amps are the choice brand for achieving that L.A. tone associated with Larry Carlton, Robben Ford, and other Gibson 335 players. Top-notch solid-state amps used by many a jazz guitarist include the Polytone Mini-Brute, Roland Jazz Chorus and the various Walter Woods models.

Experiment with as many guitar/amp configurations as you can: What works for others might not work for you. And after all, we all have different preferences as for what is a "great jazz guitar tone."

Gibson ES-175 guitar with Fender blackface
Deluxe Reverb amp.

Benedetto Manhattan guitar with
Polytone Mini-Brute amp.

TECHNIQUE

Joe Pass once said, "I don't play anything that requires abnormal stretches—you don't need to strain yourself to play jazz." He's right. Good technique is about being able to physically play what you want, or what you hear, *comfortably*.

The basics of technique vary from player to player. Some methods lend themselves to a certain jazz style; some are simply different ways to achieve the same end. Below are a few acceptable ways to play jazz guitar. Choose and develop what feels and sounds best to you. Be patient with yourself, and give your fingers, wrists, and mind time to develop.

Alternate Picking

There are different schools of alternate picking—those who prefer to attack the string dead on, and those who prefer to attack the string using a circular motion—but the idea is the same. By striking notes in strict down and up alternation, you can play faster, with less effort. It's a matter of science—less motion equals less time elapsed.

It takes practice to develop synchronization between your right and left hands. One of the best places to begin is picking the notes of a major scale, like the example below. Watch your picking hand closely: How much of it moves when you're playing? Ideally, most of the motion should be narrowed down to just the two digits holding the pick—your thumb and first finger. Concentrate on minimizing the motion. The less your wrist and arm are involved, the more efficient your overall picking motion will be. Another point to address is whether or not your picking hand is anchored on the body of the guitar; it should be. Supporting your hand somehow—whether by planting your pinky on the pickguard or resting the heel of your hand on the bridge—is crucial to gaining control.

Economy Picking

Although alternate picking is arguably the most versatile picking method, it may be beneficial to use economy picking on occasion for greater speed and fluidity. *Economy picking* incorporates successive downstrokes or upstrokes in order to travel across the strings with the least amount of movement. To illustrate, play the C major scale below, paying close attention to the picking directions. Notice the successive downstrokes and upstrokes as you transition from one string to another.

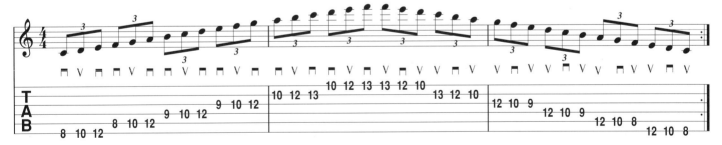

When you have this scale under your fingers using economy picking, go back and try it again using alternate picking. Notice the subtle differences? Generally speaking, economy picking is more efficient—hence the name.

Fingerstyle & Hybrid Picking

There are many schools of *fingerstyle* playing, but most jazz guitarists use their thumb and all four fingers. This approach is more common when playing chord-melody style than single-note phrases, although it can function well in both roles. Wes Montgomery, among others, was notable for his use of the thumb to articulate notes, octaves, and chords. One distinct advantage of this style is that fingers generally sound warmer than picks. Another advantage is that you can raise or lower the volume of individual notes in a chord. To play single-note phrases fingerstyle, most jazz players either alternate their first two fingers or alternate their thumb and second fingers. Using a *hybrid* of pick and fingers can offer the best of both worlds and is a popular choice among many jazz guitarists, including Joe Pass, Pat Metheny, and others. The pick is usually held between the thumb and first finger, and the three remaining fingers are assigned to pluck the top 3-4 strings.

CHORDS

One of the distinctive characteristics of jazz is its harmony, or chords. In contrast to most pop, rock, folk, and country songs, which use mainly three-note chords (major and minor triads, etc.), virtually all forms of jazz use chords that contain four or more different notes (seventh chords, extended chords, and altered chords). In addition, jazz progressions frequently contain many different chords and often travel through multiple key centers.

SEVENTH CHORDS

Seventh chords are comprised of four notes: the three notes of a triad plus a major or minor seventh interval. For example, if you use the C major triad (C–E–G) and add a major seventh interval (B), a C major seventh chord is formed. Likewise, if you substitute the minor, or flatted, seventh interval (B♭) for the B, you have a new seventh chord, the C7. This is also known as a dominant seventh chord

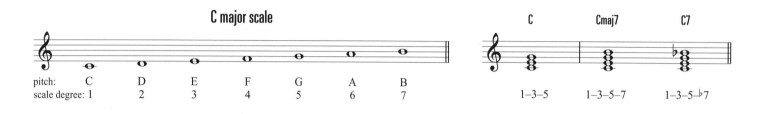

As with triads, seventh chords come in many types, including major, minor, diminished, augmented, suspended, and others. Following is a list of seventh chord types and their construction.

CHORD TYPE	FORMULA	NOTES (C AS ROOT)	CHORD NAME
major seventh	1–3–5–7	C–E–G–B	Cmaj7, CM7, C△7
dominant seventh	1–3–5–♭7	C–E–G–B♭	C7, Cdom7
minor seventh	1–♭3–5–♭7	C–E♭–G–B♭	Cm7, Cmin7, C-7
minor seven flat five (half-diminished seventh)	1–♭3–♭5–♭7	C–E♭–G♭–B♭	Cm7♭5, Cø7
diminished seventh	1–♭3–♭5–♭♭7	C–E♭–G♭–B♭♭(A)	C°7, Cdim7
augmented seventh	1–3–#5–♭7	C–E–G#–B♭	C+7, C7#5, Caug7
dominant seven flat five	1–3–♭5–♭7	C–E–G♭–B♭	C7♭5, C7(-5)
minor/major seventh	1–♭3–5–7	C–E♭–G–B	Cm(maj7), C-(maj7)

On the guitar, seventh chords can be played in a variety of locations and voicings. Below are three common fingerings for each seventh chord type. These are all *movable*—that is, they can be shifted up and down the neck and played from any root note (C, C♯, D, etc.). The root of each chord is indicated with an open circle.

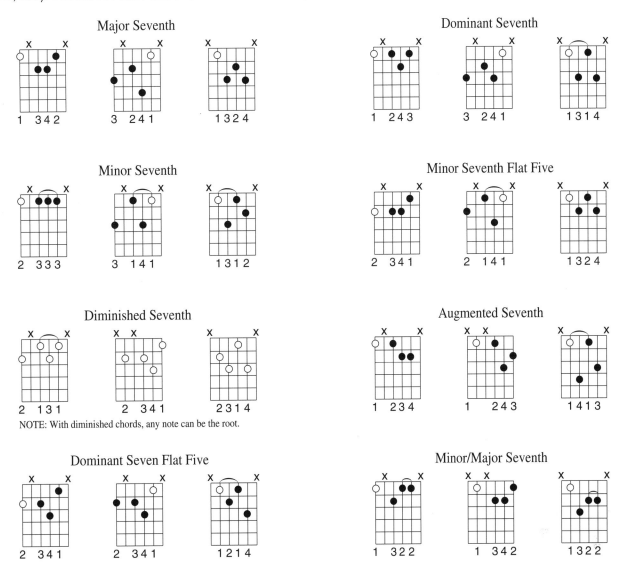

Major Seventh

1 3 4 2   3 2 4 1   1 3 2 4

Dominant Seventh

1 2 4 3   3 2 4 1   1 3 1 4

Minor Seventh

2 3 3 3   3 1 4 1   1 3 1 2

Minor Seventh Flat Five

2 3 4 1   2 1 4 1   1 3 2 4

Diminished Seventh

2 1 3 1   2 3 4 1   2 3 1 4

NOTE: With diminished chords, any note can be the root.

Augmented Seventh

1 2 3 4   1 2 4 3   1 4 1 3

Dominant Seven Flat Five

2 3 4 1   2 3 4 1   1 2 1 4

Minor/Major Seventh

1 3 2 2   1 3 4 2   1 3 2 2

Refer to this fretboard diagram if you need help finding a root or to study the notes within a chord shape.

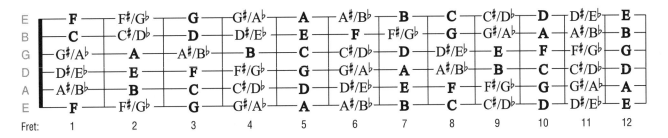

	Fret: 1	2	3	4	5	6	7	8	9	10	11	12
E	F	F♯/G♭	G	G♯/A♭	A	A♯/B♭	B	C	C♯/D♭	D	D♯/E♭	E
B	C	C♯/D♭	D	D♯/E♭	E	F	F♯/G♭	G	G♯/A♭	A	A♯/B♭	B
G	G♯/A♭	A	A♯/B♭	B	C	C♯/D♭	D	D♯/E♭	E	F	F♯/G♭	G
D	D♯/E♭	E	F	F♯/G♭	G	G♯/A♭	A	A♯/B♭	B	C	C♯/D♭	D
A	A♯/B♭	B	C	C♯/D♭	D	D♯/E♭	E	F	F♯/G♭	G	G♯/A♭	A
E	F	F♯/G♭	G	G♯/A♭	A	A♯/B♭	B	C	C♯/D♭	D	D♯/E♭	E

TECHNIQUE TIP

All of the chords above use four notes, leaving two unused strings. If you're playing with a pick, strum through all six strings while carefully muting the unused strings with your left hand. If you're playing fingerstyle, simply pluck the desired strings with your right hand while using your left hand to mute the unused strings from ringing.

Try using the seventh chords you just learned to play the following progressions. Concentrate on switching smoothly from chord to chord. For your right hand, choose a comfortable rhythm—four "strums" per measure might be a good start. Avoid strumming the chords à la pop, rock, folk, country, etc. Rather, cleanly attack the strings with downstrokes only, or pluck the notes together with your pick and fingers (hybrid picking) to simulate a pianistic effect.

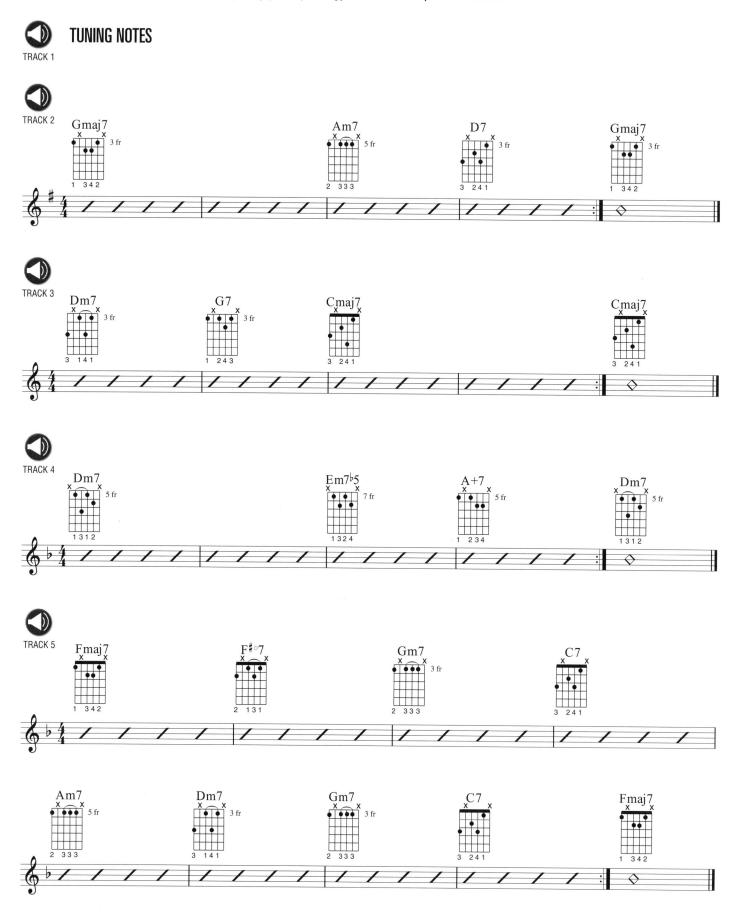

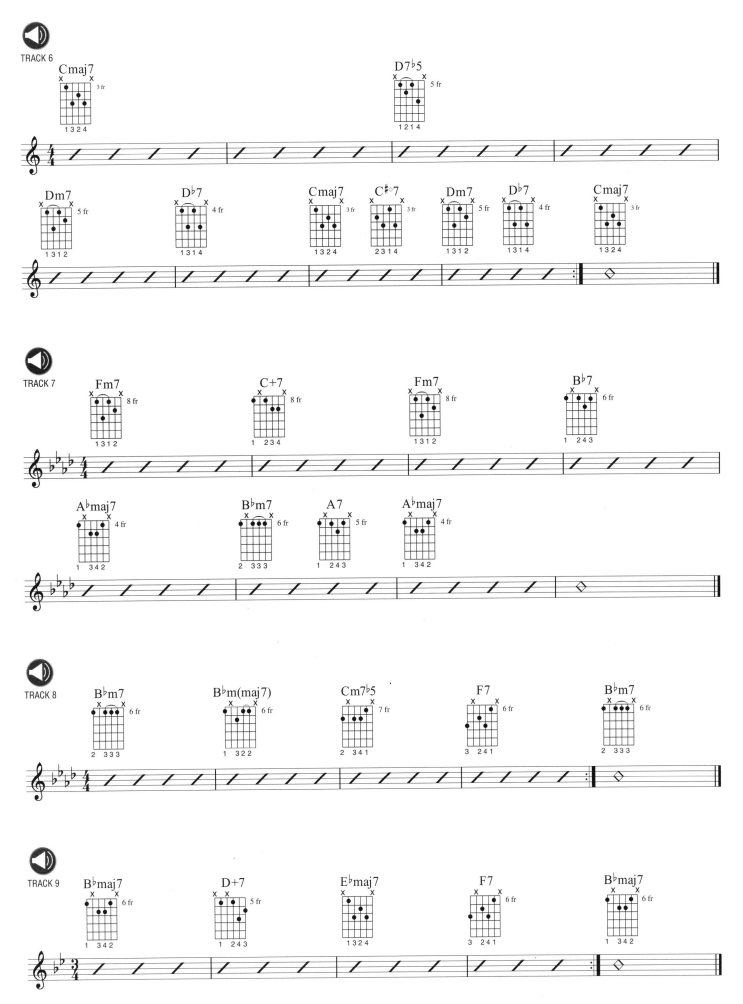

For additional chord practice, try playing these progressions again but with different voicings. Follow the chord symbols, but choose different shapes (from the ones on page 9) and strive for efficiency of movement from one chord shape to the next.

EXTENDED CHORDS

Extended chords are those that include notes beyond the seventh scale degree. For example, if you take a C dominant seventh chord and add a major ninth interval (D), you get a C dominant ninth chord (C–E–G–B♭–D). Extended chords include ninth, eleventh, and thirteenth chords. These chords have a rich, complex sound that is well-suited for jazz. Following is a list of extended chords and their construction.

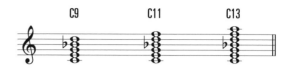

CHORD TYPE	FORMULA	NOTES (C AS ROOT)	CHORD NAME
major ninth	1–3–5–7–9	C–E–G–B–D	Cmaj9, CM9, C△9
dominant ninth	1–3–5–♭7–9	C–E–G–B♭–D	C9, Cdom9
minor ninth	1–♭3–5–♭7–9	C–E♭–G–B♭–D	Cm9, Cmin9, C-9
dominant eleventh	1–3–5–♭7–9–11	C–E–G–B♭–D–F	C11, Cdom11
minor eleventh	1–♭3–5–♭7–9–11	C–E♭–G–B♭–D–F	Cm11, Cmin11, C-11
major thirteenth	1–3–5–7–9–11–13	C–E–G–B–D–F–A	Cmaj13, CM13, C△13
dominant thirteenth	1–3–5–♭7–9–11–13	C–E–G–B♭–D–F–A	C13, Cdom13
minor thirteenth	1–♭3–5–♭7–9–11–13	C–E♭–G–B♭–D–F–A	Cm13, Cmin13, C-13

You will not likely come across a major eleventh chord;* the dissonance produced by the major 3rd against the 11th sounds rather unpleasant. For the same reason, the 11th degree is routinely omitted from major thirteenth chords.

Below are two common fingerings for each extended chord type. Notice that every fingering may not include every chord tone. Some notes may be omitted for ease of playing; the most commonly omitted note is the 5th.

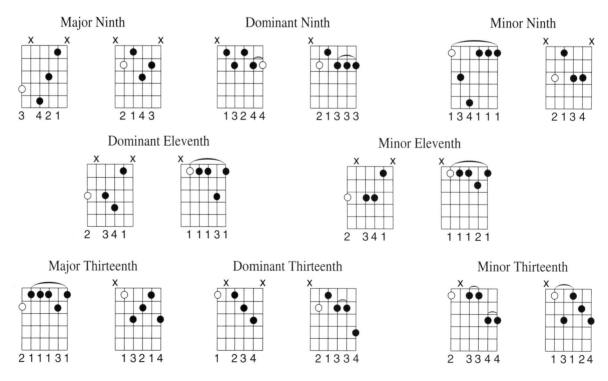

* In almost all instances, a major nine sharp eleventh (an altered chord—see pp. 14-16) will be used instead.

Now try some progressions that use extended chords.

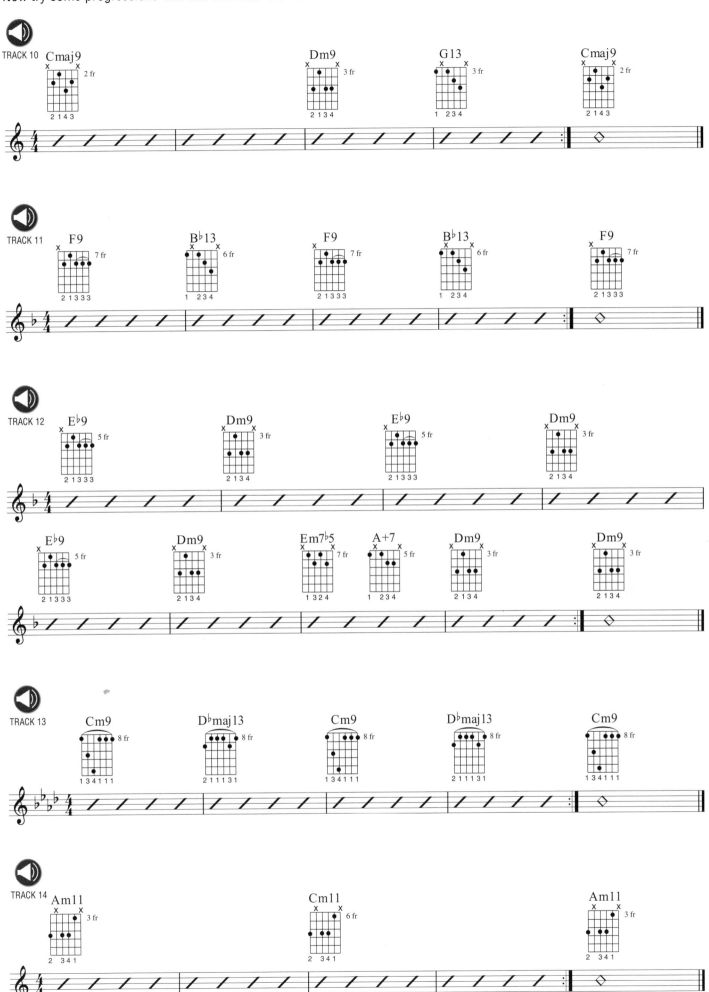

ALTERED CHORDS

Altered chords contain one or more notes that have been raised or lowered chromatically. The altered notes are usually the 5th, 9th, 11th, or 13th. Altered chords can be used to create tension, add dissonance, or facilitate smooth voice leading.

Following is a list of altered chords and their construction.

CHORD TYPE	FORMULA	NOTES (C AS ROOT)	CHORD NAME
dominant seven flat five	1–3–♭5–♭7	C–E–G♭–B♭	C7♭5, C7(-5)
dominant seven sharp five (a.k.a. augmented seventh)	1–3–♯5–♭7	C–E–G♯–B♭	C+7, C7♯5, Caug7
dominant seven flat nine	1–3–5–♭7–♭9	C–E–G–B♭–D♭	C7♭9, C7(-9)
dominant seven sharp nine	1–3–5–♭7–♯9	C–E–G–B♭–D♯	C7♯9, C7(+9)
dominant seven flat five flat nine	1–3–♭5–♭7–♭9	C–E–G♭–B♭–D♭	C7$^{♭9}_{♭5}$, C7♭5(♭9), C7($^{-9}_{-5}$)
dominant seven sharp five sharp nine	1–3–♯5–♭7–♯9	C–E–G♯–B♭–D♯	C7$^{♯9}_{♯5}$, C+7♯9, C7♯5(♯9)
dominant seven flat five sharp nine	1–3–♭5–♭7–♯9	C–E–G♭–B♭–D♯	C7$^{♯9}_{♭5}$, C7♭5(♯9)
dominant seven sharp five flat nine	1–3–♯5–♭7–♭9	C–E–G♯–B♭–D♭	C7$^{♭9}_{♯5}$, C+7♭9, C7♯5(♭9)
dominant seven sharp eleven	1–3–5–♭7–♯11	C–E–G–B♭–F♯	C7♯11, C7(+11)
dominant nine flat five	1–3–♭5–♭7–9	C–E–G♭–B♭–D	C9♭5, C9(-5)
dominant nine sharp five	1–3–♯5–♭7–9	C–E–G♯–B♭–D	C9♯5, C+9, C9(+5)
dominant nine sharp eleven	1–3–5–♭7–9–♯11	C–E–G–B♭–D–F♯	C9♯11, C9(+11)
dominant thirteen flat nine	1–3–5–♭7–♭9–11–13	C–E–G–B♭–D♭–F–A	C13♭9, C13(-9)
dominant thirteen sharp nine	1–3–5–♭7–♯9–11–13	C–E–G–B♭–D♯–F–A	C13♯9, C13(+9)
dominant thirteen sharp eleven	1–3–5–♭7–9–♯11–13	C–E–G–B♭–D–F♯–A	C13♯11, C13(+11)
minor seven flat five (a.k.a. half diminished seventh)	1–♭3–♭5–♭7	C–E♭–G♭–B♭	Cm7♭5, C-7♭5, Cø7
minor seven sharp five	1–♭3–♯5–♭7	C–E♭–G♯–B♭	Cm7♯5, C-7♯5
major seven flat five	1–3–♭5–7	C–E–G♭–B	Cmaj7♭5, C△7♭5, CM7♭5
major seven sharp five	1–3–♯5–7	C–E–G♯–B	Cmaj7♯5, C△7♯5, CM7♯5
major seven sharp eleven	1–3–5–7–♯11	C–E–G–B–F♯	Cmaj7♯11, C△7♯11, CM7♯11
major nine sharp eleven	1–3–5–7–9–♯11	C–E–G–B–D–F♯	Cmaj9♯11, C△9, CM9♯11

Following are two common fingerings for each altered chord type. Again, observe that every note need not be included in every voicing. Playability and voice leading (movement from one chord to the next) are often considerations in this regard. The most essential chord tones are generally the altered note, the 7th, and the 3rd.

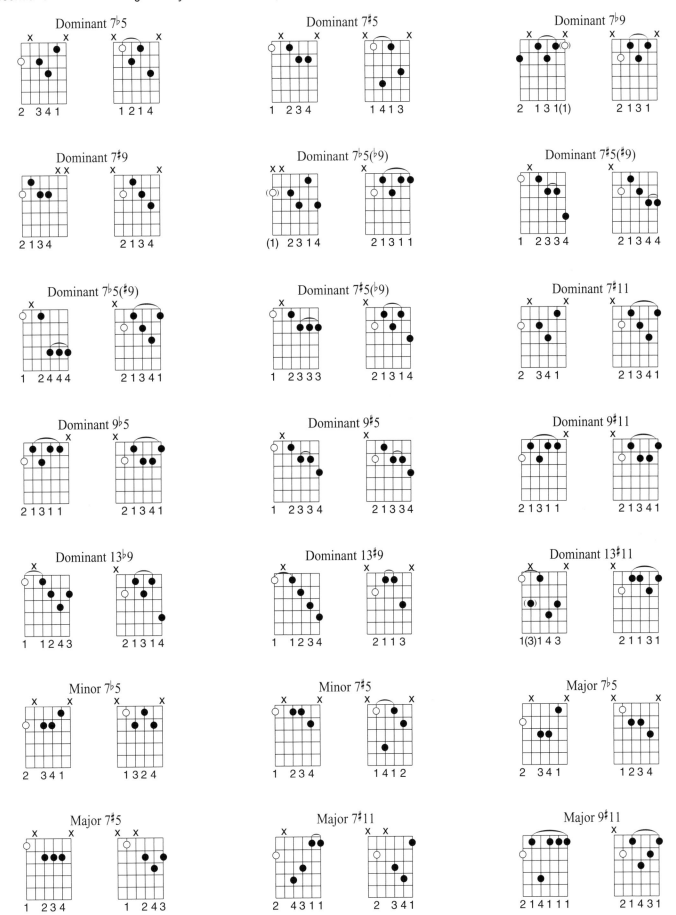

NOTE: Dominant 7♭5 and Minor 7♭5 chords were shown previously (on pages 8-9) because they are used so frequently in jazz. They are included again here for completeness.

Now try some progressions that use altered chords.

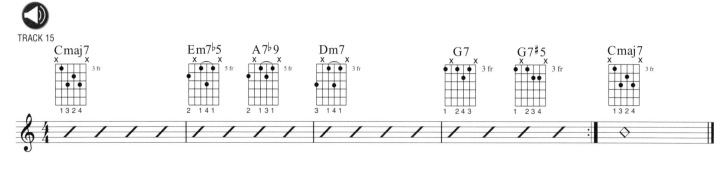

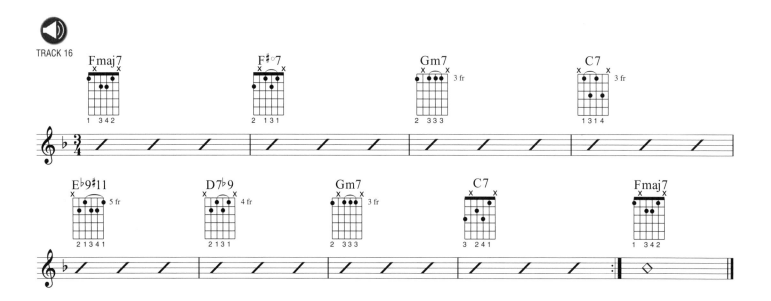

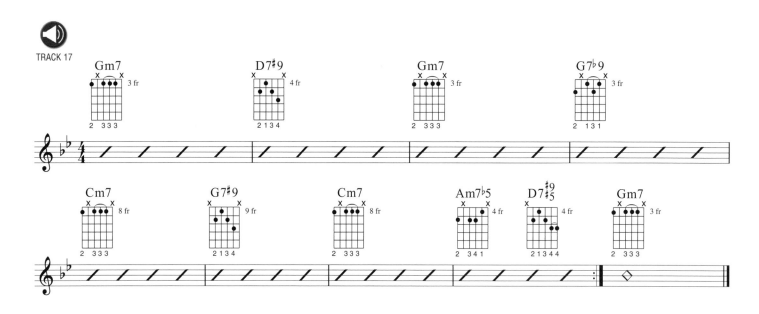

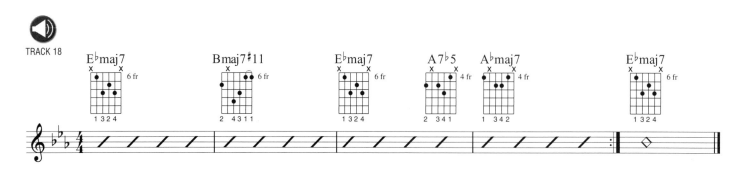

OTHER COMMON CHORDS

Below are some frequently used jazz chords that you've not learned up to this point.

The Sixth Chord

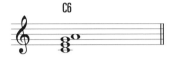

The *sixth* chord is created by adding a 6th to a major triad. This is the equivalent of stacking a major 2nd on top of the chord. The sixth chord is a good substitute chord for the major seventh, especially if the root is in the melody. It is also used to create motion by alternating with the major seventh chord in situations where the same major chord is played for a long time.

The Minor Sixth Chord

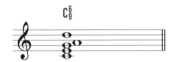

The *minor sixth* chord is created by adding a 6th to a minor triad. It has a dark, bitter sound. The minor sixth chord is a good substitute chord for the minor seventh. It is also used to create motion by alternating with the minor seventh chord in situations where the same minor chord is played for a long time.

The Six-Nine Chord

The *six-nine* chord is created by adding a 6th and 9th to a major triad. The seventh is not included. The six-nine chord is a colorful substitute for the major seventh.

Sus Chords

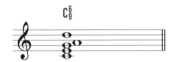

In *sus* chords, you replace the 3rd of a chord with the 4th, as in sus4, or sometimes with the 2nd, as in sus2 (pronounced "suss four" and "suss two"—the abbreviation "sus" is short for "suspended"). The resulting sound is incomplete or unresolved and has an interesting quality that is neither major nor minor. The *suspended seventh* chord is made up of the 1st, 4th, 5th, and $\flat$7th scale degrees. It is often used as a substitute chord for the dominant eleventh.

Add Chords

An *add* chord is simply a basic triad (such as a major chord) to which you add an extra note. If you take a C chord and add a D note to it, for example, you have a Cadd2 chord (with notes C–D–E–G). This chord is different than Csus2, which has no E. Add chords are typically used more in a contemporary jazz setting than in traditional jazz.

Slash Chords

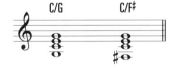

Sometimes a chord symbol ends with a slash mark (/) and an extra letter, like this: C/G (pronounced "C over G"). *Slash* chords are used to specify a bass note other than the root of the chord. To the left of the slash is the chord itself; to the right of the slash is the bass note for that chord. Often, these bass notes are tones of the chord, such as a 3rd, a 5th, or a 7th, though they may be notes outside the chord instead. C/F♯, for instance, would be a polychord that contains a bass note not otherwise belonging to the chord.

Slash chords are generally only necessary if the note in the bass is particularly important—if it belongs to a descending bass line, for instance—or if the note does not normally belong in the chord and is necessary for the overall sound. Guitarists should attempt to play the chord with the bass note on the bottom of the voicing. If this is impractical, you may ignore the note to the right of the slash and just play the chord. (When playing in a combo, be aware that the bassist will often play this note.)

The chart below is a construction summary of the chords introduced on the previous page.

CHORD TYPE	FORMULA	NOTES (C AS ROOT)	CHORD NAME
sixth	1–3–5–6	C–E–G–A	C6
minor sixth	1–♭3–5–6	C–E♭–G–A	Cm6, C-6
sixth, added ninth	1–3–5–6–9	C–E–G–A–D	C6/9, C$^6_9$
suspended second	1–2–5	C–D–G	Csus2
suspended fourth	1–4–5	C–F–G	Csus4, Csus
dominant seventh, suspended fourth	1–4–5–♭7	C–F–G–B♭	C7sus4, C7sus
added ninth	1–3–5–9	C–E–G–D	Cadd9, C(add9)
minor, added ninth	1–♭3–5–9	C–E♭–G–D	Cm(add9)

Below are two common fingerings for each chord type.

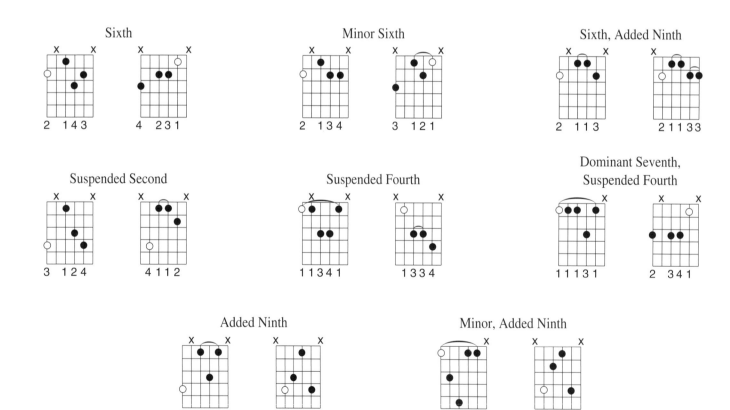

NOTE: Slash chords are not displayed above due to the abundance of construction variations and fingerings. See the next page for a few common usages.

Now try applying the chords you just learned to some common jazz progressions.

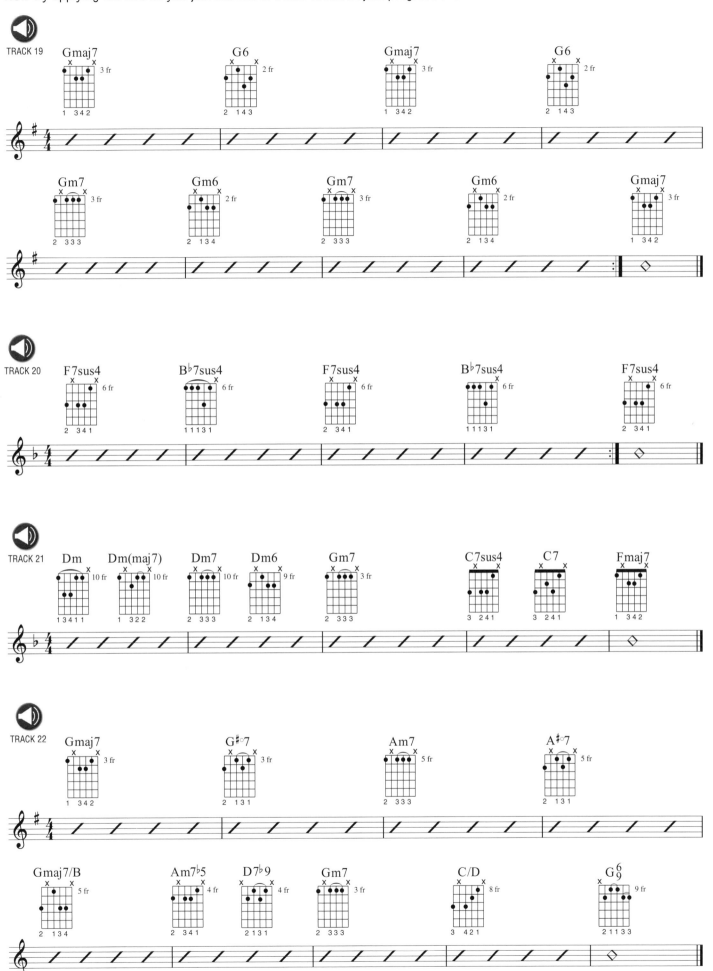

MELODY VOICINGS

Jazz guitar chords can be divided into two categories: *rhythm voicings* and *melody voicings*. Rhythm voicings, like the ones you've learned so far, usually contain a lower "bass" note on either the fifth or sixth string, and three higher notes. They offer a full-sounding chord, desirable in most comping (short for "accompaniment") situations. Conversely, melody voicings are higher register voicings. They appear primarily as closed (or adjacent) set chords on strings 1-4. Due to the lack of a lower bass note, these voicings produce a thinner, brighter sound. Melody voicings are also used for comping, especially in combos that include piano; they're less obtrusive and tend to mesh better. Melody voicings are essential to unaccompanied, solo guitar playing (a.k.a. "chord-melody" guitar).

Following are some common closed voicings for most of the chords you've leaned so far.* Once again, root notes are indicated with circles so that you can easily maneuver each voicing to any key.

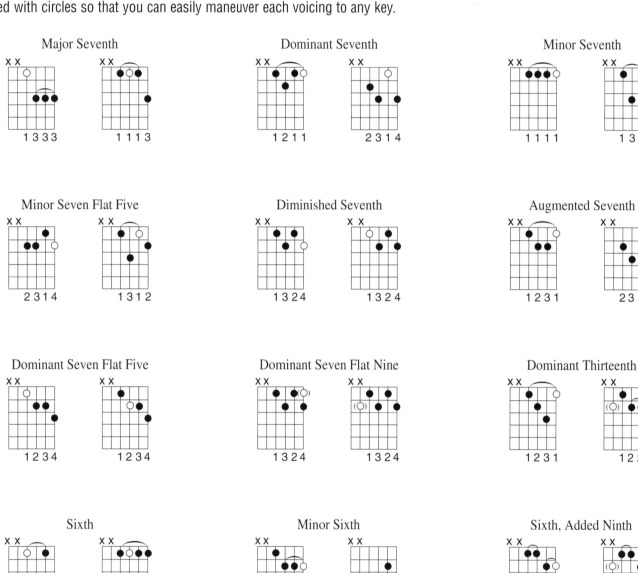

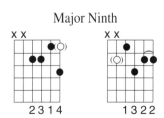
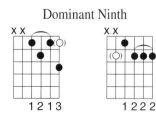
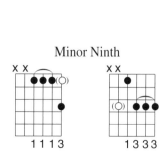

---

*For additional melody voicings, see page 68.

Practice using the melody voicings you just learned to play the following examples. Feel free to vary your rhythms; listen to the CD tracks as a guide.

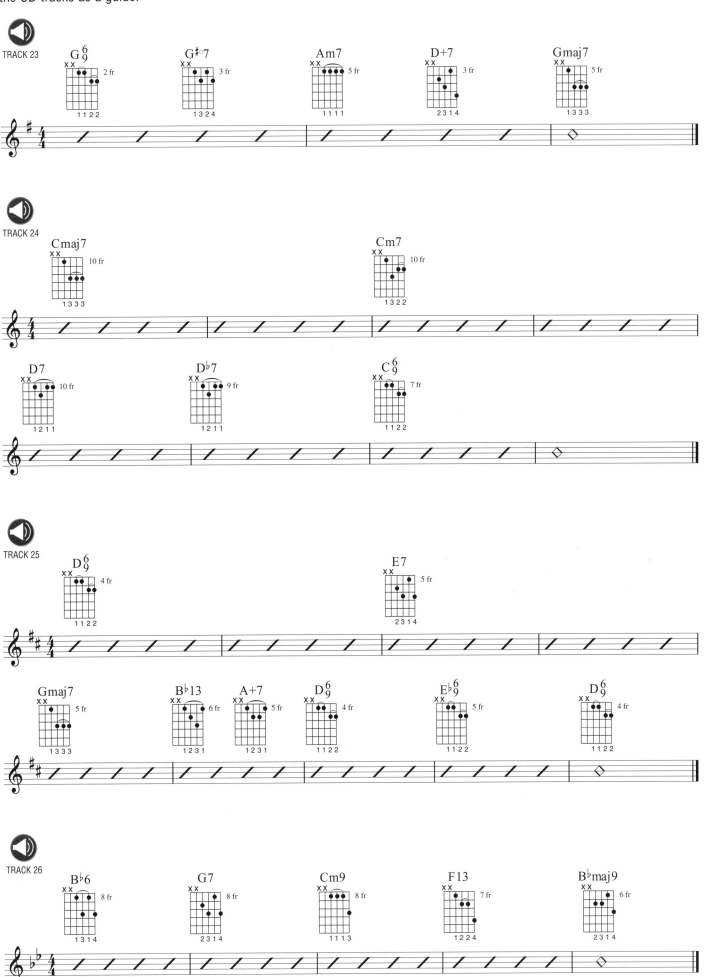

QUARTAL VOICINGS

Quartal voicings, or fourth voicings, are formed by stacking fourths instead of thirds.

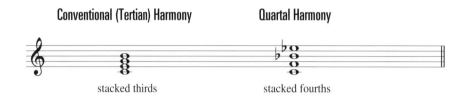

The tonality of fourth voicings is ambiguous. They are used to create tension and are especially common in bebop, fusion, and modal jazz.

Quartal chords built exclusively with fourths are call *pure fourths.* These voicings may typically be substituted for minor chords.

Minor

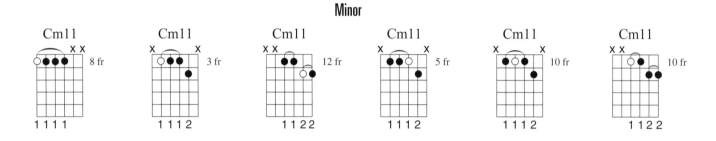

Quartal chords built with fourths plus another interval are called *diatonic fourths.* The additional interval is necessary in order to stay within the bounds of a diatonic key. These voicings may typically be substituted for major or dominant chords.

Major

Dominant

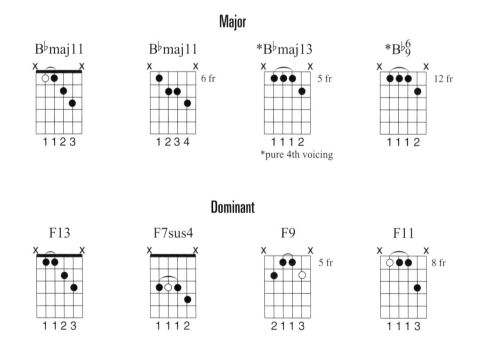

MULTI-PURPOSE VOICINGS

By now, you've discovered that playing jazz guitar requires a large vocabulary of chords. A trick that can be helpful is understanding how one single voicing can function as several different chords, depending on which note is considered to be the root. Learning to see and use these multi-purpose voicings can take a while, but once you do, your chord lexicon will quickly expand. Check out the examples below, and look around for other multi-purpose voicings on your own.

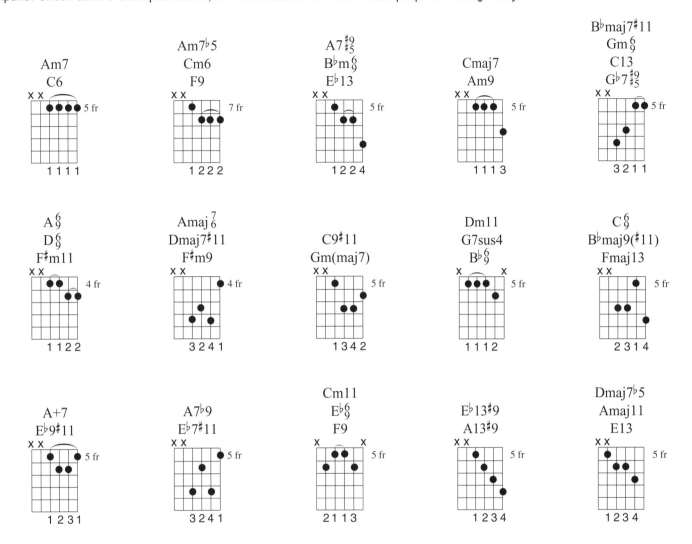

CHORD SYNONYMS

A closely related idea to multi-purpose voicings is the concept of *chord synonyms*—that is, two or more chords that have the same note spelling. The only difference between two such chords is which note is considered to be the root; as such, they are often substituted for one another. Below are a few of the most common chord synonyms, which you'll also find among the multi-purpose voicings above.

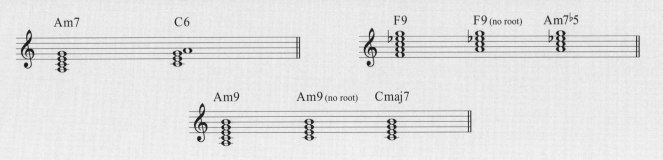

READING CHORD CHARTS

Most of the sheet music you encounter will provide chord symbols written above the song's melody. Generally, it's up to the guitarist to determine the chord voicing and rhythm. In many cases, such as when reading from a lead sheet, the chord symbols will be very basic—mostly seventh chords with no extensions or alterations. In other cases, such as when reading from a big band chart, the chord symbols will be very exact—many extended chords and alterations may be used to convey the harmony of the overall ensemble.

Whether the given chord symbols are very basic or exact, you always have the option to either *enhance* or *reduce* the chords you play. To most jazz musicians, all the chords within a given quality (major, minor, dominant, etc.) are interchangeable. Let's take a closer look.

Chord Enhancement

Jazz guitarists frequently make use of extended chords—9ths, 11ths, 13ths—and altered chords to enhance the basic seventh chords given in the lead sheet. This is called *direct substitution,* and is accomplished by replacing one chord with another chord having the same root and tonality. That is, rather than playing Gm7-to-C7 as the chart reads, you might instead play Gm9-to-C13. The chart below shows a listing of chord types, along with their possible direct substitutions. Remember: start simply; you don't need to enhance each and every chord with an extension. Direct substitution is for convenience as much as for applying fresh harmonies.

BASIC CHORD	DIRECT SUBSTITUTION
maj7	maj6, maj9, maj13, maj 6/9, maj(add9)
min7	min6, min9, min11, min13, min6/9, min(add9)
dom7	dom9, dom11, dom13, dom7sus, dom7♭5, dom7♯5, dom7♭9, dom7♯5

The following examples demonstrate chord enhancement. The chord symbols on top reflect the basic "changes" given in the lead sheet. The symbols below reflect the chords actually played.

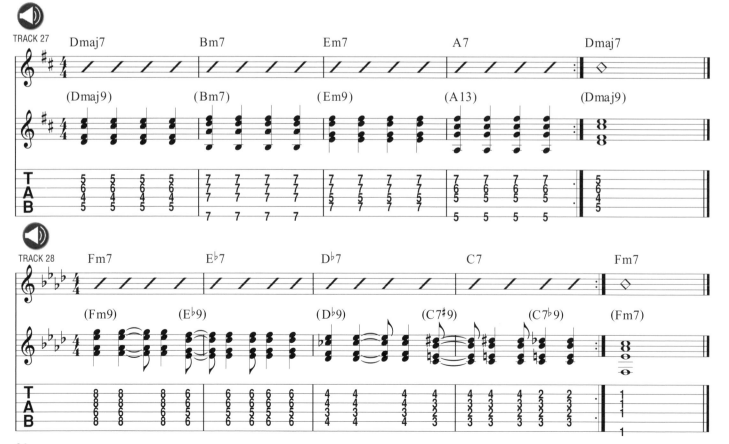

24

Chord Reduction

Chord reduction is the opposite of chord enhancement. In this case, the chart on the previous page works in reverse. If the given sheet music calls for an extended or altered chord, you may reduce this chord to its fundamental seventh chord or sixth chord. In other words, rather than play C13-to-F9 as the sheet music reads, you might instead play C7-to-F7. Again, all the chords within a given quality (major, minor, dominant) are interchangeable. Functionally, they are all the same.

The following examples demonstrate chord reduction.

When playing in a combo or big band setting, other instruments within the ensemble (e.g., piano, horn section, etc.) will often be playing the extensions or alterations. Chord reduction can simplify your part and allow more room for these other players. When reducing, you can avoid clashing with altered 5ths played by other instruments by striking only strings 4 and 3. These strings usually contain the root, 3rd, and 7th degrees.

COMMON CHORD PROGRESSIONS

It's one thing to know the chords, but it's another thing to understand their functionality. Jazz compositions can appear very complex at first, however, they can often be deduced to logical chord movements and recognizable formulae.

The ii-V

The most important progression in jazz is a minor seventh chord resolving up a 4th or down a 5th to a dominant seventh chord. This progression is known as the ii-V progression. The Roman numerals identify the chords' relationship to the key:

KEY OF C

Cmaj7	Dm7	Em7	Fmaj7	G7	Am7	Bm7♭5
	ii			V		

KEY OF F

Fmaj7	Gm7	Am7	B♭maj7	C7	Dm7	Em7♭5
	ii			V		

The ii-V progression can also be derived from minor keys:

KEY OF C MINOR

Cm(maj7)	Dm7♭5	E♭maj7♯5	Fm7	G7	A♭maj7	B°7
	ii			V		

KEY OF F MINOR

Fm(maj7)	Gm7♭5	A♭maj7♯5	B♭m7	C7	D♭maj7	E°7
	ii			V		

CIRCLE OF FIFTHS

The circle of fifths is a useful tool if you want to visualize keys and practice moving through the equivalent to consecutive ii–V progressions. Going counterclockwise takes you through the keys in 4ths: C-F-B♭-E♭-A♭-D♭, etc. This same direction also allows you to practice consecutive ii–V's. For example, you could play Cm7 to F7, Fm7 to B♭7, B♭m7 to E♭7, E♭m7 to A♭7, and so on. (You could also extend these progressions to ii–V–I's—for example, playing Cm7 to F7 to B♭maj7, Fm7 to B♭7 to E♭maj7, etc.)

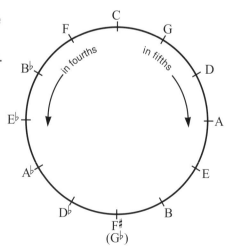

NOTE: For more on chords of a key, see pages 40-43.

Virtually every jazz composition employs a combination of ii–V progressions. Following are several typical chord patterns. The symbols underneath the staff provide a measure-by-measure analysis of the key that each chord comes from. The letter before the colon indicates the key, and the Roman numerals identify the chords' relationship to that key.

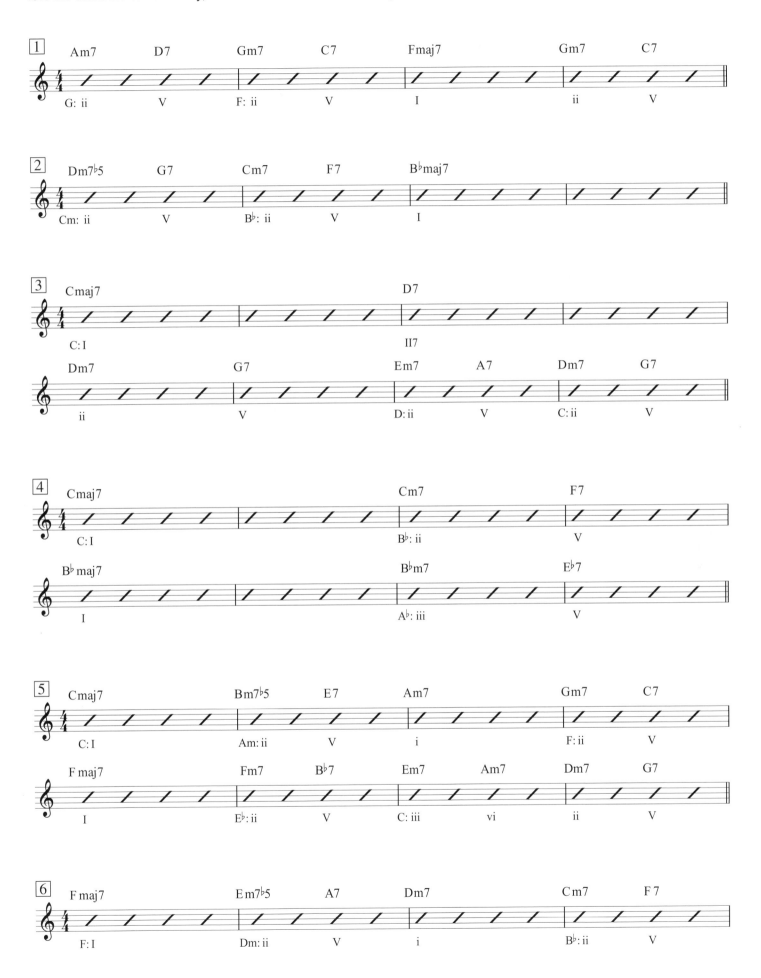

TRITONE SUBSTITUTION

Jazz musicians frequently substitute one chord for another to create more interesting harmonies. One of the most common substitution techniques is called *tritone substitution*. Here, the concept is that V, ii (II), or vi (VI) chords traveling from V to I can be replaced with a dominant or major chord whose root is three whole steps, or tritone, away. For example, instead of A7, you can play E♭7. When moving to a I chord (Dmaj7), this creates a half-step bass motion.

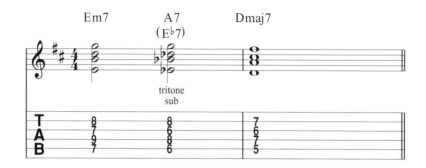

Why does this work? Well, let's look at the individual notes in each chord. A7 contains the notes A–C♯–E–G. E♭7 contains the notes E♭–G–B♭–D♭ (C♯). In essence, E♭7 can also be thought of as A7♭9♭5.

The following chord progressions make use of tritone substitution. Take a moment to compare the spelling of the original chord (labeled on top) with its tritone sub.

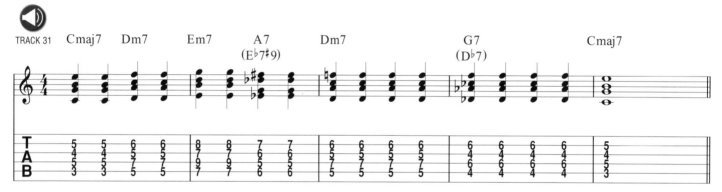

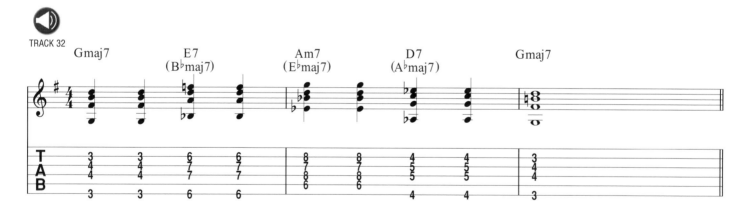

Another common form of tritone substitution incorporates "backcycling." Here, instead of playing Gm7 for one measure, C7 for one measure, and Fmaj7 for one measure, you would play Gm7 for two beats, C7 for two beats, D♭m7 for two beats, G♭7 for two beats, and Fmaj7 for one measure.

PASSING CHORDS

Passing chords are chords that are not part of a song's written harmony, but serve to connect two chords that are. Usually, they are placed either a half step above or below the destination chord, or the chord they are leading to. For instance, you can precede a Cmaj7 with either Bmaj7 or C#maj7. The technique adds harmonic color and also provides a smoother chord transition.

The following examples illustrate how passing chords can be added to common jazz progressions.

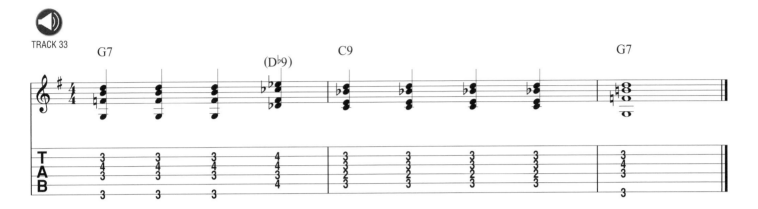

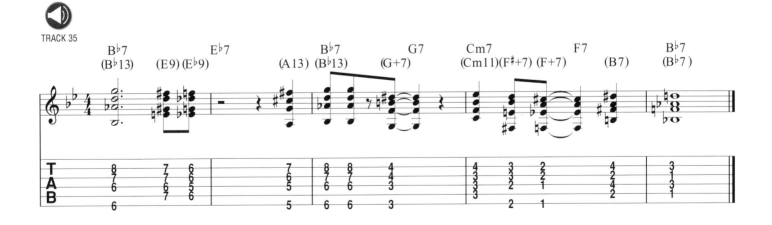

COMPING STYLES

Comping is short for "accompaniment" and refers to the technique of improvising a chordal backing in jazz. This section demonstrates six different styles of comping.

BIG BAND

The term "rhythm guitar" originated in the late 1920s during the development of the Swing era. As big bands (ensembles/orchestras of 10 pieces or more) led by Count Basie, Duke Ellington, and Artie Shaw rose to popularity in the 1930s, the guitar assumed an important role as the backbone of the rhythm section. Basie guitarist Freddie Green pioneered the "four-to-the-bar" rhythm style that soon became the distinctive sound of early jazz comping. As the name suggests, the technique employs simple quarter-note downstrums—in 4/4 time, four strums per measure, or bar. While the rest of the band swings, these steady quarter-note strums hold the rhythm section together like glue.

Green played with heavy strings and high action. He used a pick and typically brushed over the lower strings before striking the middle strings sharply. He also favored three-note voicings; in most cases, he opted to not play the top note in a standard four-note rhythm chord.

Medium Swing

Jazz music has provided a thriving foundation for an assortment of rhythmic feels. Perhaps most prominent is the swing rhythm, characterized by its uneven or "lopsided" eighth-note pulse:

Although swing initially became associated with early Kansas City and New Orleans musicians like Duke Ellington and that of Glenn Miller, as well as legendary bandleader Benny Goodman, its basic elements have become a staple in other related idioms such as Dixieland, boogie-woogie, bebop, and other post-1950s jazz off-shoots. The basic "long-short, long-short" swing phrasing is still one of the defining sounds of jazz.

Ironically, the four-to-the-bar style doesn't feature swing eighth notes—just quarter notes. The rest of the band "swings" over this foundation. The most typical comping pattern in this style features long strums on beats 1 and 3 and slightly accented staccato strums on beats 2 and 4. In big band and "society" gig settings, this pattern is sustained throughout the song (i.e., under both the melody and solos).

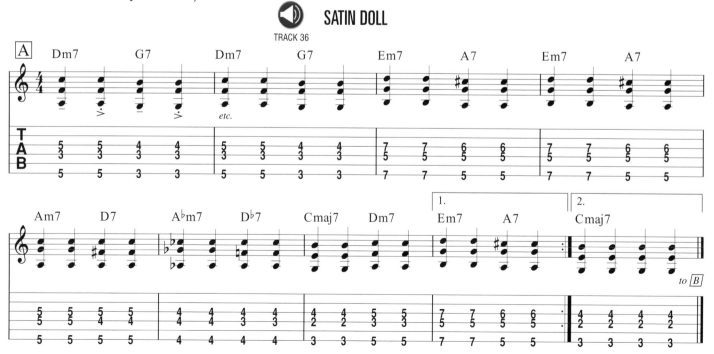

SATIN DOLL

TRACK 36

By Duke Ellington
Copyright © 1953 (Renewed 1981) and Assigned to Famous Music Corporation in the U.S.A.
Rights for the world outside the U.S.A. Controlled by Tempo Music, Inc. c/o Music Sales Corporation

Uptempo Swing

For faster tempo songs, rhythm guitarists usually employ tight, staccato strums. The shortness of the notes is controlled by the left hand releasing each chord after it is strummed. To add harmonic interest and rhythmic motion, guitarists frequently shift voicings and/or mix sixth and seventh chords with triads in situations where the same chord is written for a long time.

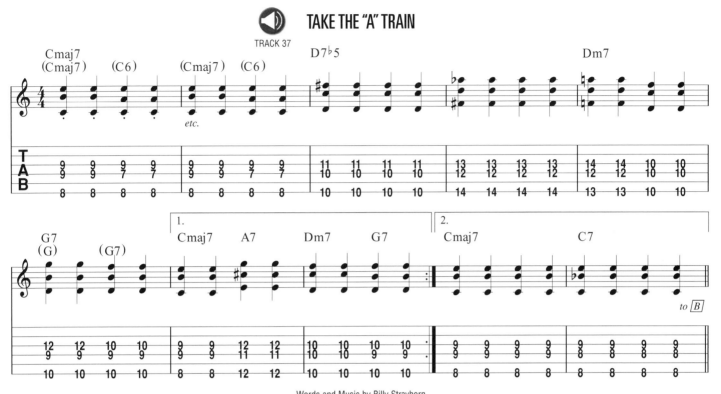

TAKE THE "A" TRAIN

TRACK 37

Words and Music by Billy Strayhorn
Copyright © 1941; Renewed 1969 DreamWorks Songs (ASCAP) and Billy Strayhorn Songs, Inc. (ASCAP) for the U.S.A.
Rights for DreamWorks Songs and Billy Strayhorn Songs, Inc. Administered by Cherry Lane Music Publishing Company, Inc.

Ballads

Another option for comping in a big band setting is to rest on beats 1 and 3 and play long strums on beats 2 and 4. This pattern is particularly common when playing ballads.

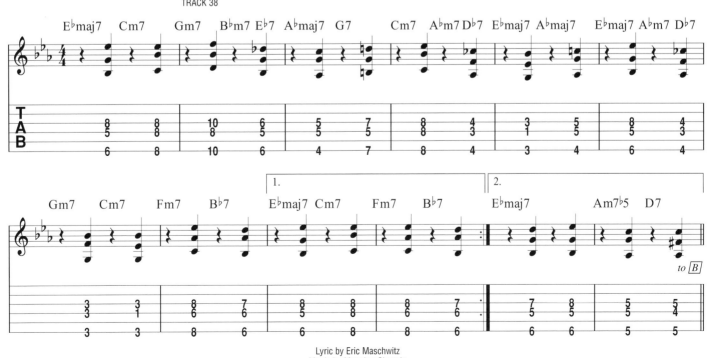

A NIGHTINGALE SANG IN BERKELEY SQUARE

TRACK 38

Lyric by Eric Maschwitz
Music by Manning Sherwin
Copyright © 1940 The Peter Maurice Music Co., Ltd., London, England
Copyright Renewed and Assigned to Shapiro, Bernstein & Co., Inc., New York for U.S.A. and Canada

SMALL COMBO

Jazz guitar comping became more liberal beginning with the impact of 1940s small-group music. Trio, quartet, and quintet settings induced guitarists to broaden their rhythmic and harmonic accompaniment. Consequently, guitarists like Tal Farlow and Barney Kessel abandoned the four-to-the-bar comping style in favor of thicker voicings and more active, often syncopated, rhythms.

The accompaniment played behind a song's melody, or "head," should complement the melody itself, both rhythmically and harmonically. The same can be said for comping behind soloists, although here your accompaniment must be improvised in order to dovetail with the lead player's rhythmic and harmonic performance. Listen closely to the dynamics and pitch register of the entire ensemble; if the solo is slowly building, stay conservative, if the solo is making use of lower pitch notes, try voicing chords higher up the neck.

Bebop Blues

"Billie's Bounce," by Charlie Parker, is an example of a bebop blues in the key of F. Notice that nearly all of the chords are either extended (9th, 11th, or 13th) or altered. You may use a pick, your fingers, or a combination of the two.

BILLIE'S BOUNCE (BILL'S BOUNCE)

TRACK 39

By Charlie Parker
Copyright © 1945 (Renewed 1973) Atlantic Music Corp.
All Rights for the World excluding the U.S. Controlled and Administered by Screen Gems-EMI Music Inc.

Modal Jazz

In the 1960s, musicians began composing songs with static chords and repeated vamps rather than moving changes. The simpler, more atmospheric framework became known as *modal jazz,* so named because improvisors experimented with playing several related scales, or modes, over a single chord. When comping behind modal compositions, guitarists favor compact voicings and flowing rhythm.

TRACK 40 **IMPRESSIONS**

By John Coltrane
Copyright © 1974 JOWCOL MUSIC

Jazz Waltz

Some jazz songs are played in 3/4 time (three quarter notes per measure). The defining characteristic of any waltz is a 3/4 time signature, however, a *jazz waltz* differs from other waltz styles in the way the beats are felt. Instead of placing the pulse, or accent, on the first beat as in a "one feel," a jazz waltz places accents on beats 1 and the "and" of 2. This is called a "two over three feel"; each measure is divided in half, resulting in two dotted quarter notes. The division of time is useful when there are two chord changes in a measure of 3/4. Another approach to comping in 3/4 time is to play a half note on beat 1 and a quarter note on beat 3.

BLUESETTE

TRACK 41

Words by Norman Gimbel
Music by Jean Thielemans
Copyright © 1963, 1964 SONGS OF UNIVERSAL, INC.
Copyright Renewed; Words Renewed 1992 by NORMAN GIMBEL for the World and Assigned to NEW THUNDER MUSIC, INC.
Administered by GIMBEL MUSIC GROUP, INC. (P.O. Box 15221, Beverly Hills, CA 90209 USA)

34

Ballads

In slower pieces, guitarists often use fuller voicings and more resonant rhythms. Don't be afraid to play a chord and let it ring for the entire measure. Occasionally, there may also be room for small fills—you can arpeggiate chords or transition through a few different voicings when there are gaps in the melody or improvisation.

Ballad tempos can range from unbearably slow to leisurely swing. They can be slightly out of time (rubato), played with even eighth notes, or have a tripletlike feel, as in a 12/8 ballad.

Here is an excerpt from a jazz standard that demonstrates ballad accompaniment.

MY ONE AND ONLY LOVE

TRACK 42

Words by Robert Mellin
Music by Guy Wood
© 1952, 1953 (Renewed 1980, 1981) EMI MUSIC PUBLISHING LTD. and WAROCK CORP.
All Rights for EMI MUSIC PUBLISHING LTD. Controlled and Administered by COLGEMS-EMI MUSIC INC.

MUST-KNOW STANDARDS

There are several hundred jazz standards. Following is an alphabetical list of arguably the most commonly played songs in four different categories.

Straight-Ahead Swing	Ballad	Waltz	Bossa Nova
1. All the Things You Are	1. Body and Soul	1. Alice in Wonderland	1. Black Orpheus
2. Autumn Leaves	2. Here's That Rainy Day	2. All Blues	2. Blue Bossa
3. The Days of Wine and Roses	3. In a Sentimental Mood	3. Bluesette	3. The Girl from Ipanema
4. A Foggy Day	4. Misty	4. Falling in Love with Love	4. How Insensitive
5. Have You Met Miss Jones?	5. My Foolish Heart	5. Fly Me to the Moon	5. Recorda-me
6. Just Friends	6. My Funny Valentine	6. Footprints	6. The Shadow of Your Smile
7. My Romance	7. My One and Only Love	7. My Favorite Things	7. Song for My Father
8. Satin Doll	8. 'Round Midnight	8. Someday My Prince Will Come	8. So Nice (Summer Samba)
9. Stella by Starlight	9. When I Fall in Love	9. Tenderly	9. Watch What Happens
10. There Will Never Be Another You	10. When Sunny Gets Blue	10. Windows	10. Wave

Latin Jazz

Latin music has been a constant influence on jazz since the 1940s, when musicians from Cuba, Puerto Rico, and South America began to incorporate an even eighth-note feel to the existing sensibilities of American jazz. "Latin" has since become a very generic term in jazz circles, usually meaning a derivative of bossa nova or samba, both styles from Brazil. Brazilian guitarist/ composer Antonio Carlos Jobim emerged as the undisputed champion of Latin jazz as he rendered a string of hits, including "The Girl from Ipanema," "Wave," "Corcovado," and "Desafinado." Trumpeter Dizzy Gillespie and other American musicians brought the Afro-Cuban influence into modern jazz, and most current groups continue to allocate a portion of their repertoire to the Latin style. Rhythm guitar accompaniments in this style feature heavy syncopation (striking chords "off the beat").

The gentle *bossa nova* beat uses even eighth notes and lots of syncopation. Its tempo is usually between 110 and 150 beats per minute. Most guitarists strum with all downstrokes or use their pick and fingers to pluck the strings simultaneously. Following are four common bossa nova comping patterns.

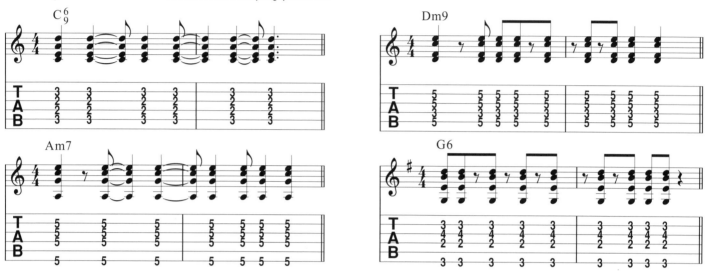

Now try playing the written accompaniment to the first 16 measures of the bossa nova standard "Desafinado."

DESAFINADO

TRACK 43

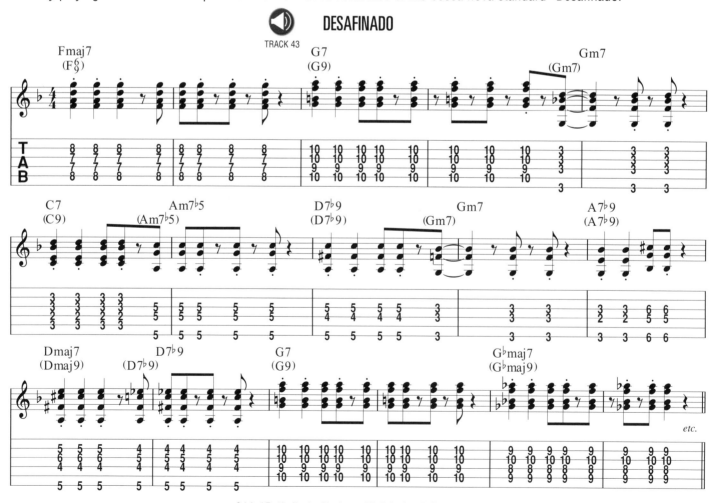

etc.

To jazz musicians, the *samba* is simply a bossa nova played much faster. Guitarists typically comp using steady up- and down-strokes in an eighth-note rhythm; some strums are accented and others are muted, usually at random.

Following are two common samba comping patterns. Note that you may streamline these patterns when playing sambas that are very fast.

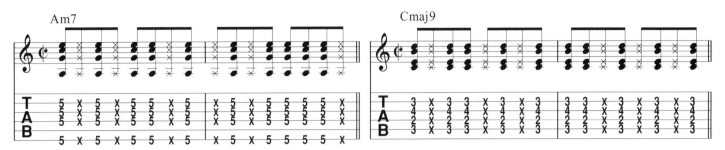

Use the first pattern shown above to play the Latin standard "Samba De Orfeu."

SAMBA DE ORFEU

TRACK 44

etc.

Words by Antonio Maria
Music by Luiz Bonfa
Copyright © 1959 by Nouvelles Editions Meridian
Copyrights for the United States of America and Canada Renewed and Assigned to Chappell & Co. and United Artists Music Co., Inc.
All Rights Administered by Chappell & Co.

IMPROVISATION

At the heart of jazz is *improvisation*. By definition, jazz improvisation is the spontaneous and unrehearsed expression of musical ideas. Virtually all jazz songs offer space for musicians to showcase their abilities to ad-lib a solo.

Improvisors generally gain their unique voice through the personal quirks of their tone and timing. That is, both note choice and phrasing play a key role in how interesting an improvised statement is. Listening to great soloists like Pat Martino, Johnny Smith, Charlie Christian, Joe Pass, and many others is invaluable. Meanwhile, studying lines from horn players like Charlie Parker, Coleman Hawkins, and John Coltrane is also a tradition crucial to fully understanding the idiom.

As clichéd as it might sound, playing a solo is like telling a story. In order to convey a good story, you need to know what you're talking about. This means you must know the chords over which you'll be improvising as well as the scales that correspond to them. A *scale* is a series of notes arranged in a specific order or pattern. For every chord, there is at least one scale that works well for improvisation. Jazz music makes use of many different scales, including the major scale (and its modes), the harmonic minor scale, the melodic minor scale, the diminished scale, the whole tone scale, and others. Understanding the construction of these scales, their positions on the fretboard, and their relationship to chords is crucial. The following pages explain in detail these basic relationships.

THE MAJOR SCALE

Perhaps the most common scale is the *major scale*. It's the basis for countless melodies, riffs, solos, and chord progressions.

Construction

Scales are constructed using a combination of whole steps and half steps. (Remember: on the guitar, a half step is the distance of one fret; a whole step is two frets.) All major scales are built from the following step pattern.

WHOLE – WHOLE – HALF – WHOLE – WHOLE – WHOLE – HALF

This series of whole and half steps gives the major scale its characteristic sound. To build a C major scale, start with the note C and follow the step pattern above.

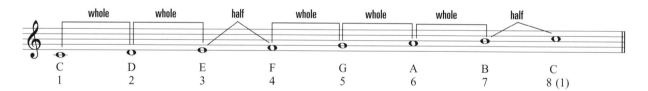

The first (and eighth) degree of a major scale is called the *tonic*, or root. This is the "home" tone on which most melodies end.

To build a G major scale, start with the note G and apply the major-scale step pattern. The F is sharped to complete the pattern.

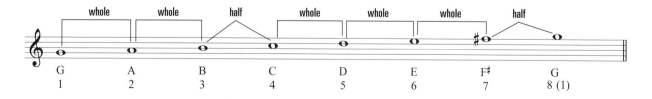

The major scale step pattern can be applied to any root note to create any major scale. If you start on D, you will have a D major scale: D-E-F#-G-A-B-C#-D. If you start on E, you will have an E major scale: E-F#-G#-A-B-C#-D#-E. If you start on F, you will have an F major scale, and so on.

---

* The following pages move ahead with the presumption that you understand the basics of how scales are constructed. If you need more help with respect to either scales or keys, please see the *Incredible Scale Finder* (00695490), also published by Hal Leonard Corporation as a supplement to the Hal Leonard Guitar Method.

Fingerings

Scale patterns played on the guitar typically cover all of the notes within a certain fretboard area. In other words, the notes of the scale are played through more than one octave for a more complete and practical fingering. To become a skillful soloist and proficient all-around guitarist, you must learn to play scales anywhere on the fingerboard. All of the scale patterns in this book are *movable*—that is, they can be shifted up and down the neck to accommodate any key. Simply match one of the roots to its respective note on the fingerboard, and the rest of the pattern follows accordingly.

Memorize the three movable major scale patterns below. (Roots are indicated with an open circle.) Then study the diagrams at the right, which illustrate how all three patterns link up on the fretboard—first in the key of G and then in the key of C.

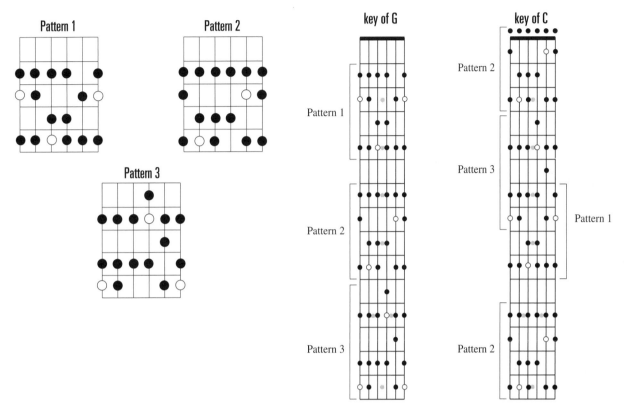

The scale patterns above each stay within a specific four- or five-fret position. There are many more patterns you could learn, and this could take you months, maybe years. In time, it would be a very good idea for you to work up some more fingerings in various areas of the fingerboard.

Below are two G major scale patterns that differ from those above. The first spans six frets and consists of *three-notes-per-string*. The second spans seventeen frets and consists of four-notes-per-string; this type of horizontal scale pattern can be handy when trying to connect distant areas of the fretboard or to smoothly transfer from one position to another. Try applying these types of alternative fingering patterns with other scales introduced on the following pages.

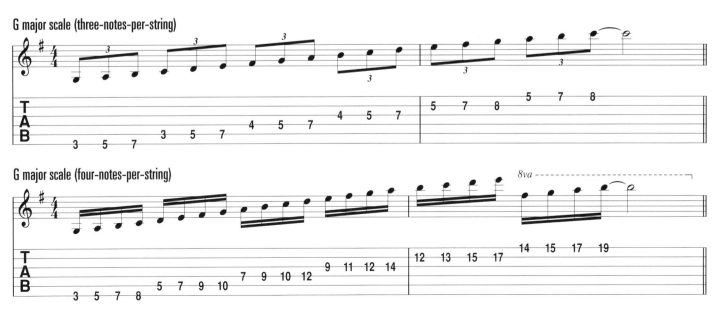

Chords of the Major Scale

Chords and chord progressions are also derived from scales. A piece of music based on the C major scale is in the key of C major. For every key, there are seven corresponding chords—one built on each note of the major scale.

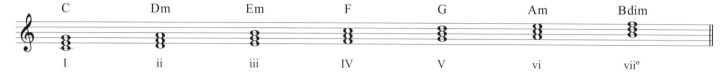

By taking a closer look at each of the seven chords, notice that major triads are built on the first, fourth, and fifth notes of the scale; minor triads are built on the second, third, and sixth notes of the scale; and a diminished triad is built on the seventh note of the scale. The seven chords are common to the key of C because all seven contain only the notes of the C major scale (no sharps or flats). It is important to memorize this sequence of chord types, as it applies to all major scales.

Of course, most jazz chord progressions contain seventh chords instead of triads. The seventh chords built on the notes of the C major scale are:

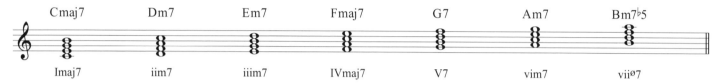

The secret to effectively applying scales to chords is knowing how chords can be grouped together so that one scale can be used to improvise over a series of chord "changes." Most jazz compositions segue through multiple keys; however, by using the theory of chord-scale relationships introduced above it is often possible to organize a few consecutive chords into one tonal center. This will enable you to improvise over these chords without needing to change scales.

The next two chord progressions are in the key of C. Record yourself playing the chords, then play the progression back and use the C major scale to improvise. Play the scale ascending and descending and notice how the notes work over the chords. Later, try to mix up the notes.

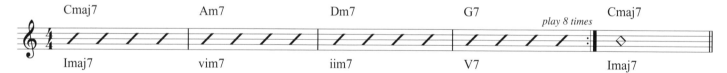

The next chord progression is also in the key of C, however, it is slightly disguised by the presence of extended chords. Extended chords function in keeping with the chord family they are derived from. For example, a Cmaj9 chord is an extension of C. Similarly, G9, G11, and G13 are all part of the dominant chord family, and function in the same way that a plain G7 chord would.

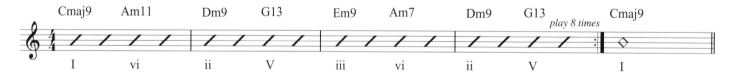

IMPROV TIPS

- **Cling to the Chords** – Emphasize the notes of each chord being played.

- **Less is More** – Choose your notes carefully; sometimes it's not the quantity but the quality.

- **Work the Rhythm** – Use syncopation, triplets, and repeating patterns to help make your solos interesting and distinctive.

- **Tell a Story** – Let your solo take shape with a beginning, middle, and end.

Modes of the Major Scale

Modes are scales built upon each note of a central scale. Just as there are seven notes in a major scale, there are seven modes derived from the major scale. The names of these seven modes are: Ionian, Dorian, Phrygian, Lydian, Mixolydian, Aeolian, and Locrian. It's important to point out that each of these modes is just a permutated major scale. That is, the seven modes of C major all contain the same notes; they just start and end on a different pitch.

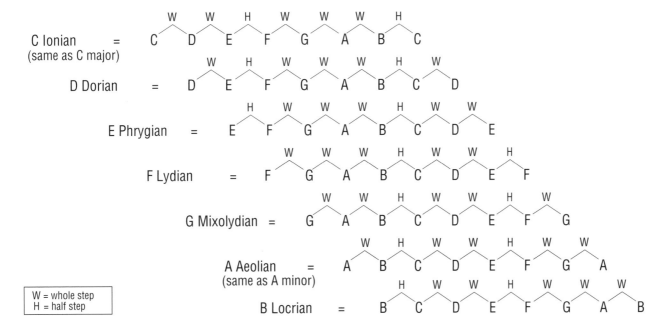

W = whole step
H = half step

Each mode of the major scale corresponds to the diatonic chord that shares the same root. The C Ionian mode could be used to improvise over Cmaj7, the G Mixolydian mode would be used over G7, the V chord, and so on. You might ask, "Aren't these modes the same as the major scale we just learned?" The answer is yes; it's just the terminology that differs. When you see a chord progression that travels from Dm7 to G7 to Cmaj7, you can think of playing C major, or you can think of playing D Dorian to G Mixolydian to C Ionian.

MORE ABOUT MODES

If you examine the chart above closely, you should notice that the whole-step/half-step intervals change from mode to mode. This provides you with yet another way to understand and analyze modes. For example, rather than seeing D Dorian and thinking of it as the second mode of C major, you could analyze D Dorian as a D major scale with flatted 3rd and flatted 7th degrees. To the right are the scale formulas necessary to generate each of the seven modes using this method.

This way of thinking of modes may allow you to hear and better understand the sounds that various modes produce. For example, in situations where one chord, Dm7, is played for a long time, you may improvise using D Dorian, D Phrygian, or D Aeolian.

IONIAN:	1–2–3–4–5–6–7
DORIAN:	1–2–♭3–4–5–6–♭7
PHRYGIAN:	1–♭2–♭3–4–5–♭6–♭7
LYDIAN:	1–2–3–♯4–5–6–7
MIXOLYDIAN:	1–2–3–4–5–6–♭7
AEOLIAN:	1–2–♭3–4–5–♭6–♭7
LOCRIAN:	1–♭2–♭3–4–♭5–♭6–♭7

Here are two movable fingerings for all seven major modes:

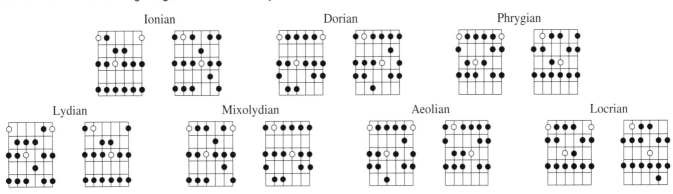

Ionian   Dorian   Phrygian

Lydian   Mixolydian   Aeolian   Locrian

THE HARMONIC MINOR SCALE

The *harmonic minor scale* has been used for centuries in many different contexts. Its unique construction produces many interesting sounds and makes it a frequent and compelling choice among jazz musicians.

Construction

The step pattern for the harmonic minor scale is whole–half–whole–whole–half–whole+half–half. To build a C harmonic minor scale, start with the note C and follow the pattern accordingly:

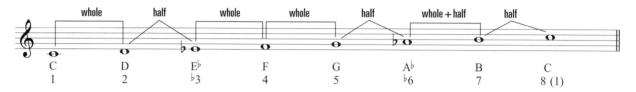

The harmonic minor scale can also be thought of as a major scale with flatted 3rd and 6th degrees, or a natural minor scale with a raised 7th degree.

Chords

The seventh chords built on the C harmonic minor scale are:

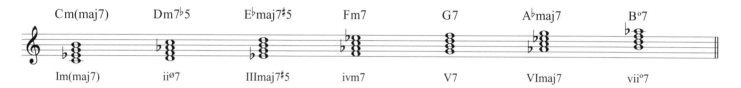

Modes

In jazz music, the modes of the harmonic minor scale—especially the second, fifth, and seventh—are used very often. Here are two movable fingerings for each mode of the harmonic minor scale.

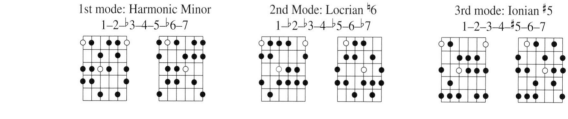

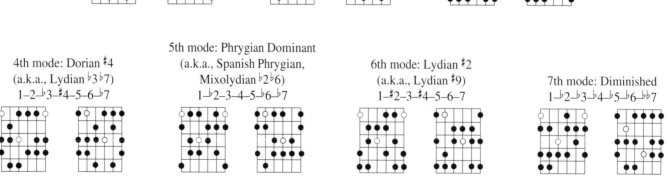

THE MELODIC MINOR SCALE

The *melodic minor scale* is commonly referred to as the "jazz minor scale." Its distinctive character generates many familiar jazz sounds. In fact, the melodic minor scale is used by jazz musicians as frequently as the major scale.

Construction

The step pattern for the melodic minor scale is whole–half–whole–whole–whole–whole–half. To build a C melodic minor scale, start with the note C and follow the pattern accordingly:

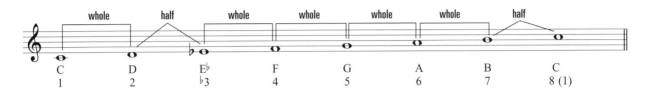

The melodic minor scale can also be thought of as a major scale with a flatted 3rd degree, or a natural minor scale with raised 6th and 7th degrees.

Chords

The seventh chords built on the C melodic minor scale are:

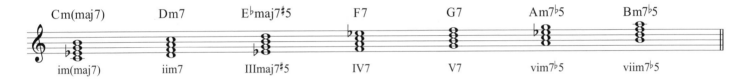

Modes

In jazz music, the modes of the melodic minor scale—especially the fourth, sixth, and seventh—are used very often. Here are two movable fingerings for each mode of the melodic minor scale.

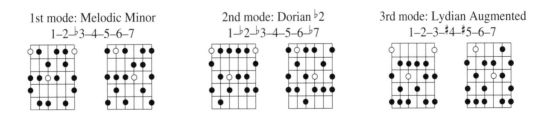

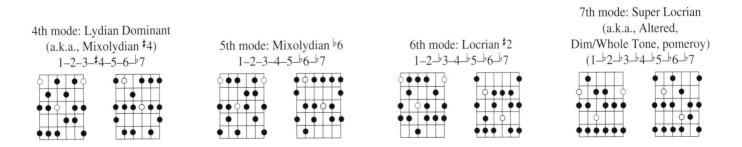

THE DIMINISHED SCALE

The *diminished scale* is a symmetrical scale built from alternating whole steps and half steps. This alternating pattern results in two variations: the *whole-half* and the *half-whole*.

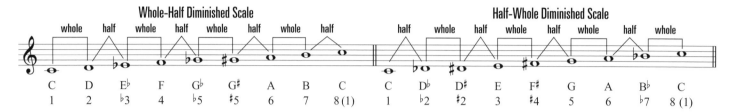

Notice that these scales repeat themselves every time they are played a minor 3rd higher. As a result, the C diminished scale contains the same notes as the E♭ (D♯), G♭ (F♯), and A diminished scales; the C♯ (D♭) diminished scale contains the same notes as the E, G, and B♭ (A♯) diminished scales; and the D diminished scale contains the same notes as the F, A♭ (G♯), and B diminished scales.

Here are two movable fingerings for each version of the diminished scale.

Whole-Half Diminished Scale
1–2–♭3–4–♭5–♯5–6–7–1

Half-Whole Diminished Scale
(a.k.a., Dominant Diminished Scale)
1–♭2–♯2–3–♯4–5–6–♭7–1

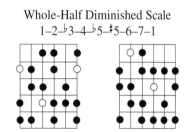
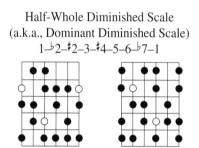

THE WHOLE TONE SCALE

The *whole tone scale* is a symmetrical scale built entirely of whole steps, or whole tones.

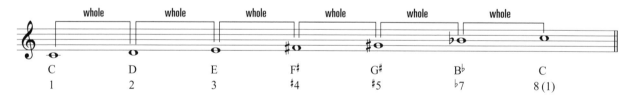

Notice that this scale repeats itself every time it is played a whole step higher. As a result, the C whole tone scale contains the same notes as the D, E, F♯ (G♭), G♯ (A♭), and A♯ (B♭) whole tone scales. Likewise, the C♯ (D♭) whole tone scale contains the same notes as the D♯ (E♭), F, G, A, and B whole tone scales.

Here are two movable fingerings for the whole tone scale.

Whole Tone Scale

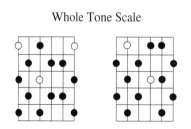

IMPROVISING OVER DOMINANT CHORDS

There are seven different scales that work well over dominant chords. Following is an explanation of when and how each scale is used, along with common licks to both help illustrate the resulting sounds and develop your vocabulary.

Mixolydian (1-2-3-4-5-6-♭7)

TRACK 45

The *Mixolydian* mode is best suited for playing over unaltered dominant chords (e.g., 7th, 9th, 11th, 13th). It effectively complements these chords in both *cadential*, or functioning, harmonic progressions (such as a resolving V–I progression) and *non-cadential,* or non-functioning, harmonic progressions (such as a non-resolving V–IV progression).

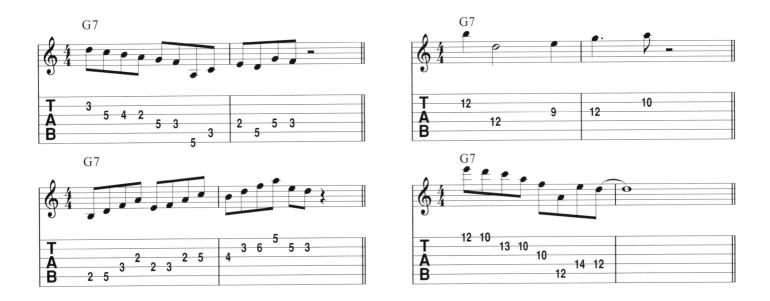

Phrygian Dominant (1-♭2-3-4-5-♭6-♭7)

TRACK 46

Phrygian dominant, the V mode of harmonic minor, is best suited for playing over 7♭9, 7♯9, or 7♭9♯9 chords. It also works well over unaltered dominant chords. The scale is usually used in cadential harmonic progressions that resolve to either a im7 or Imaj7 chord.

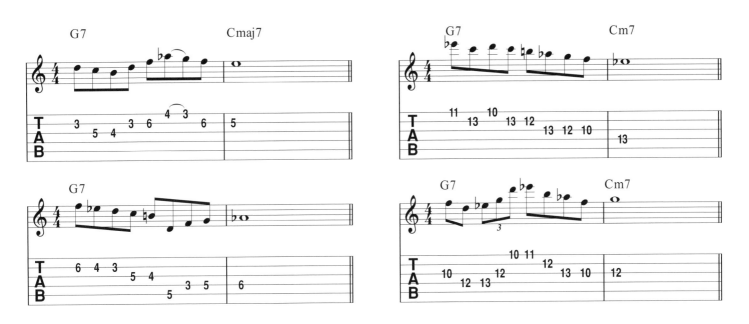

Lydian Dominant (1-2-3-#4-5-6-♭7)

The *Lydian dominant* scale (a.k.a. Mixolydian #4) is best suited for playing over 7#11, or 7♭5, chords. It also works well over unaltered dominant chords. The scale is usually used in non-cadential harmonic progressions.

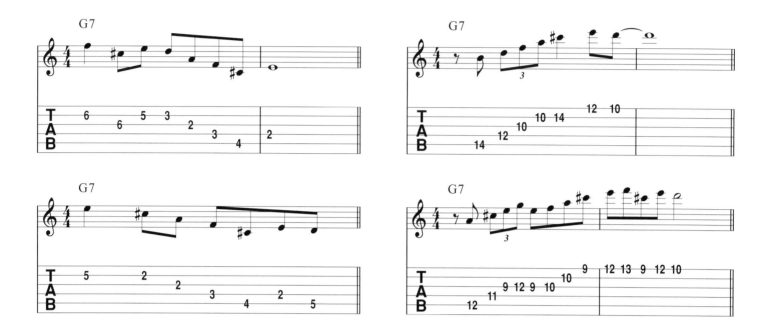

Super Locrian (1-♭2-♭3-♭4-♭5-♭6-♭7)

The *super Locrian* scale (a.k.a. the altered scale) is best suited for playing over altered dominant chords (e.g., 7#9, 7#5, 7♭9, 7♭5, 7#9/♭5, 7♭9/♭5, 7#9/#5, 7♭9/#5). Since the alterations create so much dissonance, the scale is almost always used in cadential, or resolving harmonic progressions.

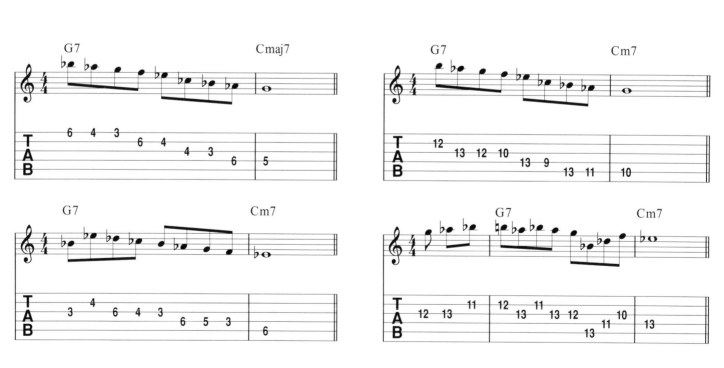

Dominant Diminished (1-♭2-♯2-3-♯4-5-6-♭7)

TRACK 49

The *dominant diminished* scale (a.k.a. half-whole diminished) is best suited for playing over chords with ♭5, ♭9, and ♯9 alterations. It also works well over unaltered dominant chords. The scale is usually used in cadential harmonic progressions.

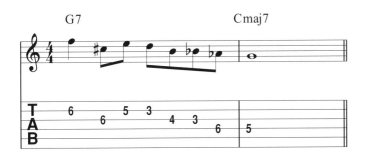

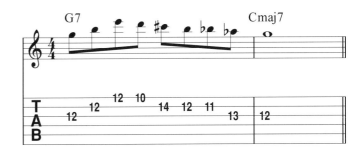

Whole Tone (1-2-3-♯4-♯5-♭7)

TRACK 49
cont'd

The *whole tone* scale is best suited for playing over 7♯5 chords, but it also works well over unaltered dominant chords. The scale can be used in both cadential and non-cadential harmonic progressions.

Mixolydian ♭6 (1-2-3-4-5-♭6-♭7)

TRACK 49
cont'd

Mixolydian ♭6, the V mode of melodic minor, is best suited for playing over 7♯5 and 9♯5 chords (note that the 9th degree should not be altered). It also works well over unaltered dominant chords. The scale can be used in either cadential or non-cadential harmonic progressions.

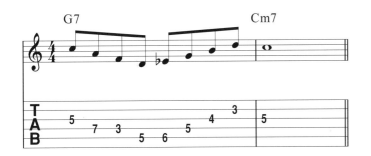

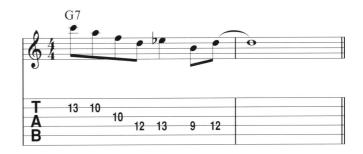

IMPROVISING OVER MAJOR CHORDS

There are three different scales that work well over major chords. Following is an explanation of when and how each scale is used, along with common licks to help illustrate the resulting sounds and develop your vocabulary.

Ionian (1-2-3-4-5-6-7)

TRACK 50

The *Ionian* mode, a.k.a. the major scale, is best suited for playing over maj7, maj9, and maj13 chords. Note that the scale's 4th degree is often avoided—that is, it is sometimes played but rarely emphasized.

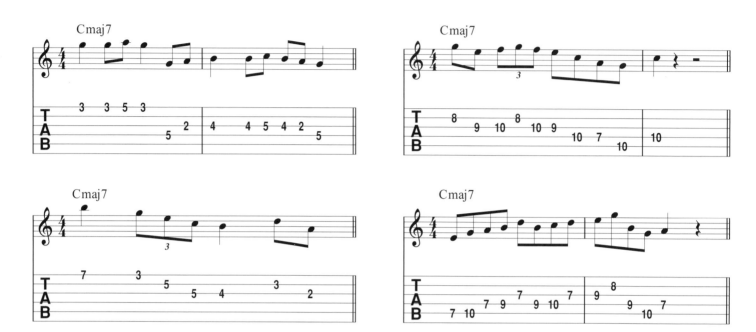

Lydian (1-2-3-#4-5-6-7)

TRACK 51

The *Lydian* mode is best suited for playing over maj7#11 chords, but it also works well over maj7, maj9, and maj13 chords.

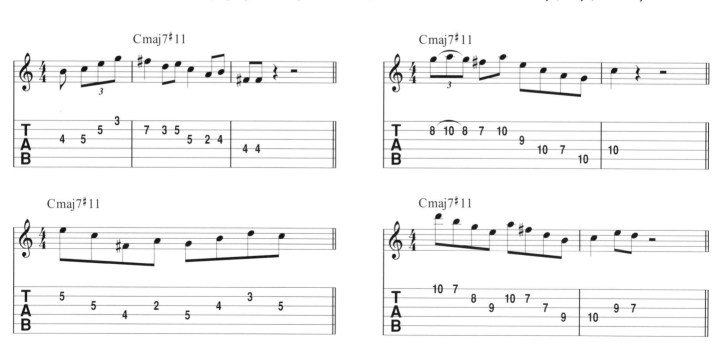

Lydian ♯2 (1-♯2-3-♯4-5-6-7)

The *Lydian ♯2* scale, the VI mode of harmonic minor, is best suited for playing over maj7♯11 chords, but it also works well over maj7, maj9, and maj13 chords.

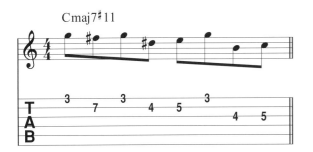

MELODIC EMBELLISHMENTS

Passing Tones

Just as English grammar uses labels such as "conjunction," "preposition," and "pronoun" to indicate a part of speech or some other functional classification, music has its own terminology to identify compositional and improvisational techniques. By definition, *passing tones* are not part of the song's harmony but serve to connect two notes that are. For example, if you played the notes C–C♯–D over a Cmaj13 chord, C♯ would be considered a passing tone. The lick below is a typical phrase in the jazz lexicon that uses passing tones chromatically. Notice that the passing tones themselves, which are circled, fall on the upbeat, or the weak part of the beat. In general, this is the best spot to place them into the fabric of your lines.

When passing tones are positioned chromatically within a phrase, as in the phrase above, they are sometimes referred to as "chromatic passing tones." However, the term *chromaticism* is a much broader expression that describes the use of any notes outside the song's key—not necessarily between two chord tones.

Neighbor Tones & Surround Tones

While we're on the subject, you should also become familiar with two more labels: neighbor tones and surround tones. A *neighbor tone* is a nonharmonic note on the weak beat that moves a half or whole step above (or below) another note and then returns to that note. *Surround tones* are notes that combine to circle above and below a target note. They anticipate the resolution of the third note, thereby establishing the color and harmony of the ensuing chord. Check out the lick below for a sample of neighbor tones and surround tones in action.

IMPROVISING OVER MINOR CHORDS

There are seven different scales that can be played over minor chords. Two of these scales—Dorian #4 and Dorian ♭2—are used less frequently than the others and are therefore omitted from this lesson. Following is an explanation of when and how each scale is used along with common licks to both help illustrate the resulting sounds and develop your vocabulary.

Dorian (1-2-♭3-4-5-6-♭7)

TRACK 53

The *Dorian* mode is best suited for playing over m6, m7, m9, and m11 chords. It is typically employed over minor chords functioning as ii chords, but also effectively complements im7 chords.

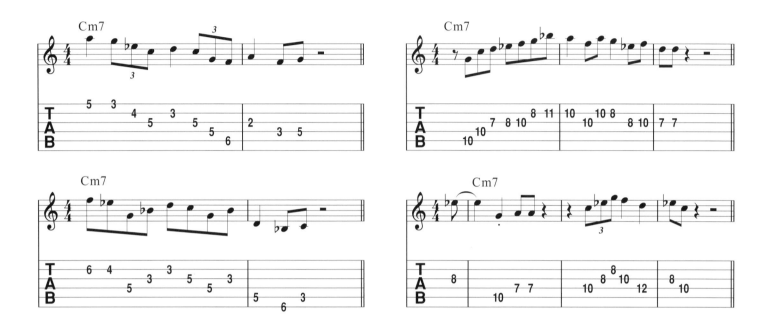

Harmonic Minor (1-2-♭3-4-5-♭6-7)

TRACK 54

The *harmonic minor* scale is generally the first choice for improvising over m(maj7), m7, m9, and m11 chords when they are functioning as a tonic i chord. Its design, however, does not effectively complement m6 chords.

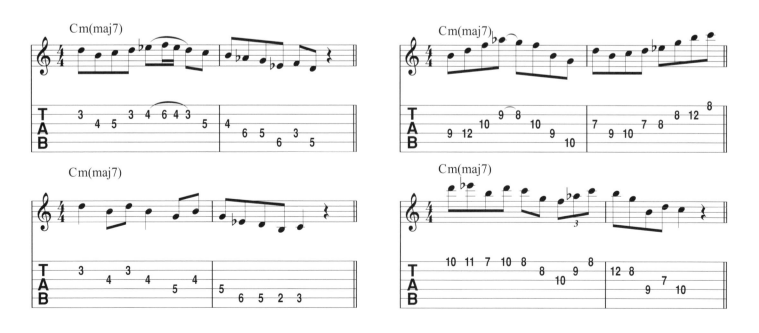

Melodic Minor (1-2-♭3-4-5-6-7)

TRACK 55

The *melodic minor* scale works best over m(maj7) and m6 chords when they are functioning as the tonic i chord but also works well over m7, m9, and m11 chords.

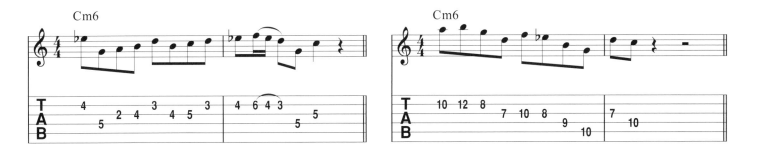

Aeolian (1-2-♭3-4-5-♭6-♭7)

TRACK 55 cont'd

The *Aeolian* mode can be used over any m7, m9, or m11 chord. It is best suited over these chords when they are functioning as vi chords. The scale should be avoided when playing over m6 chords.

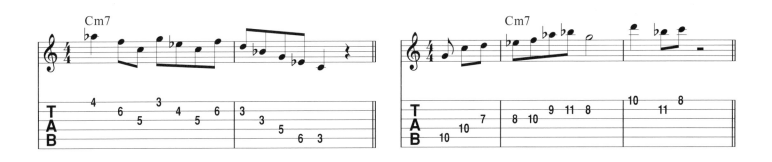

Phrygian (1-♭2-♭3-4-5-♭6-♭7)

TRACK 55 cont'd

The *Phrygian* mode is best suited for playing over m7 and m11 chords. However, it should not be used over m6 or m9 chords.

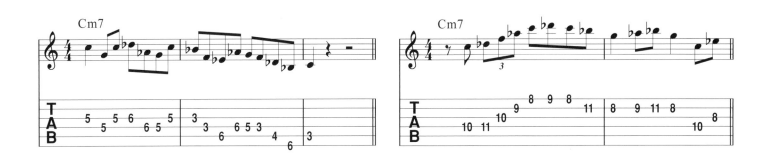

IMPROVISING OVER MINOR 7♭5 CHORDS

There are three main scales that can be played over m7♭5 chords. Once again, here is an explanation of when and how each scale is used along with a few common licks.

Locrian ♮6 (1-♭2-♭3-4-♭5-6-♭7)

TRACK 56

Locrian ♮6, a mode of harmonic minor, is most often used over a m7♭5 chord within a progression approaching the V chord (e.g., Dm7♭5–G7♭9–Cm7 or Dm7♭5–G7–Cmaj7).

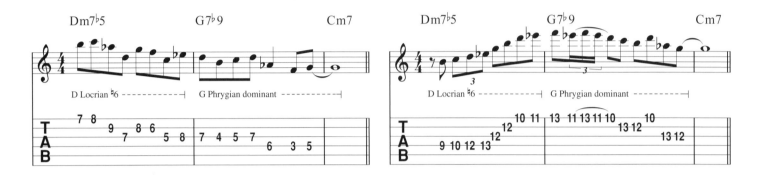

Locrian #2 (1-2-♭3-4-♭5-♭6-♭7)

TRACK 56
cont'd

Locrian #2, a mode of melodic minor, is also most often used over a m7♭5 chord within a progression approaching a V chord.

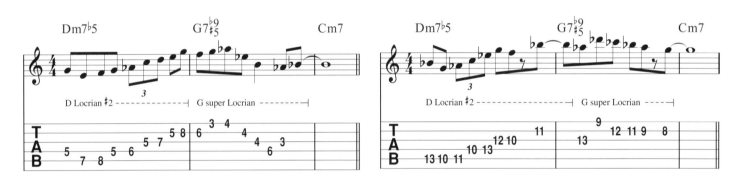

Locrian (1-♭2-♭3-4-♭5-♭6-♭7)

TRACK 56
cont'd

The *Locrian* mode is best suited for playing over a m7♭5 chord that is functioning as a vii chord. It can also be used over a m7♭5 chord that is played for a long time.

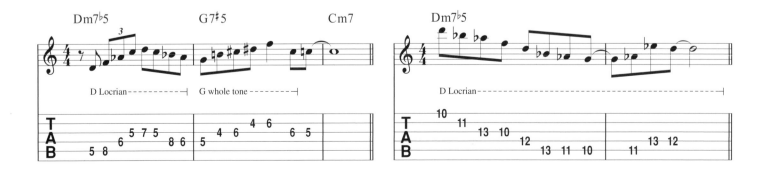

IMPROVISING OVER DIMINISHED SEVENTH CHORDS

TRACK 57

There are two different scales that can be played over diminished seventh chords. The *diminished mode* (vii of harmonic minor) is best suited over dim7 chords that resolve up a half step. The *whole-half diminished scale* works well over dim7 chords that resolve either up or down.

Diminished Mode (1-♭2-♭3-♭4-♭5-♭6-♭♭7)

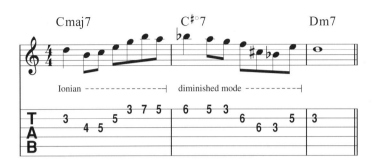

Whole-Half Diminished Scale (1-2-♭3-4-♭5-♯5-6-7)

IMPROVISING OVER MAJOR 7♯5 CHORDS

TRACK 58

There are two different scales that can be played over maj7♯5 chords: *Ionian ♯5* and *Lydian augmented* (the III modes of harmonic minor and melodic minor, respectively).

Ionian ♯5 (1-2-3-4-♯5-6-7)

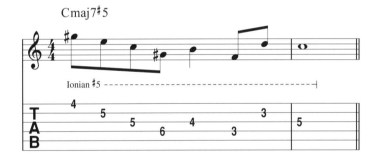

Lydian Augmented (1-2-3-♯4-♯5-6-7)

LICK SUBSTITUTION

Nearly every phrase in the jazz vocabulary can be used in multiple contexts. Use the following chart as a guide.

Play any **Dmaj7** idea over	Play any **Dm7** idea over	Play any **G7** idea over
Am7	Bm7♭5	Dm7
D13	C♯7$_{♯5}^{♭9}$	Bm7♭5
F♯m7♭5	G9	C♯7$_{♯5}^{♭9}$
Cmaj7	G11	
D7sus4	G13	
B7($_{♭5}^{♭9}$ $_{♯5}^{♯9}$)		
Fmaj♯11		

SOLOING STYLES

Single-note jazz guitar solos come in a variety of sounds and traditions. This section demonstrates eight different styles of improvisation.

EARLY SWING

Lonnie Johnson, Eddie Lang, Dick McDonough, Carl Kress, Oscar Moore, Teddy Bunn, Django Reinhardt, and Charlie Christian were the most notable guitar pioneers who cultivated jazz improvisation in the 1920s and 1930s. Typical solos from the era featured arpeggios, blues inflections, minimal altered pitches, fluid rhythmic phrasing, and a propensity to stay close to the song's melody.

HONEYSUCKLE ROSE

TRACK 59

MAINSTREAM JAZZ

The guitarists most associated with straight-ahead jazz are Barney Kessel, Johnny Smith, Wes Montgomery, Jim Hall, and Kenny Burrell. Their improvisation styles are characterized by melodic scale-like lines, keen harmonic sense, passing tones, and swinging horn-like phrasing.

Moderate Swing

"Autumn Leaves" is a classic mid-tempo jazz standard. Lay back on the eighth notes to help capture the requisite swing feel.

AUTUMN LEAVES (LES FEUILLES MORTES)
TRACK 60

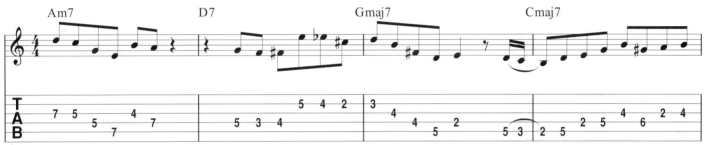

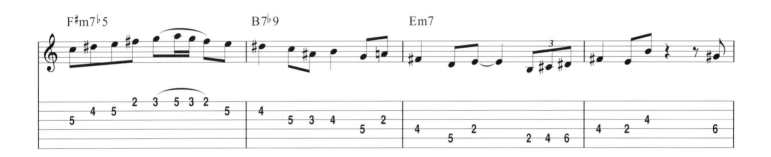

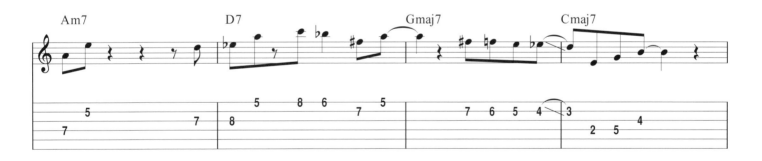

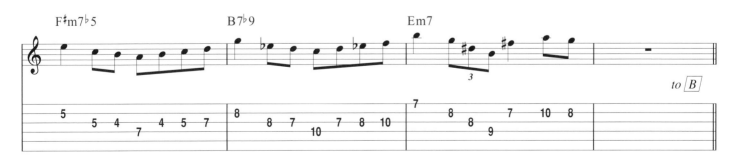

English lyric by Johnny Mercer
French lyric by Jacques Prevert
Music by Joseph Kosma
© 1947, 1950 (Renewed) ENOCH ET CIE
Sole Selling Agent for U.S. and Canada: MORLEY MUSIC CO., by agreement with ENOCH ET CIE

Bossa Nova

It's important to also develop your improvisational skills in a Latin setting. Most licks and phrases can be assimilated into the style's even eighth-note feel; however, it helps to emphasize rhythmic syncopation.

WATCH WHAT HAPPENS

TRACK 61

Music by Michel Legrand
Original French Text by Jacques Demy
English Lyrics by Norman Gimbel
Copyright © 1964 PRODUCTIONS MICHEL LEGRAND and PRODUCTIONS FRANCIS LEMARQUE
Copyright © 1965 UNIVERSAL - SONGS OF POLYGRAM INTERNATIONAL, INC. and JONWARE MUSIC CORP.
Copyright Renewed; English words Renewed 1993 by NORMAN GIMBEL and Assigned to
GIMBEL MUSIC GROUP, INC. (P.O. Box 15221, Beverly Hills, CA 90209 USA)

Ballads

Improvising over ballads can be deceptively challenging; the chord changes move slowly, but the feel and phrasing requires rhythmic command and lots of patience. Some players prefer to feel slower tempos in double time. Other players elect to balance simple phrases played "in time" with long runs played *rubato*, or "out of time."

EASY LIVING

TRACK 62

Theme from the Paramount Picture EASY LIVING
Words and Music by Leo Robin and Ralph Rainger
Copyright © 1937 (Renewed 1964) by Famous Music Corporation

BEBOP

Bebop allowed jazz improvisors to showcase their formidable technique and adventurous harmonic sense. Bop guitar stylists such as Tal Farlow and Joe Pass exhibited fleet single-note phrases, dazzling melodic invention, and lots of altered pitches.

Uptempo Bop

Charlie Parker's "Ornithology" is the quintessential bebop tune. Here is Parker's solo adapted for guitar.

ORNITHOLOGY
TRACK 63

By Charlie Parker and Bennie Harris
Copyright © 1946 (Renewed 1974) Atlantic Music Corp.

Blues

The 12-bar blues progression is used frequently in all genres of jazz; however, it is especially prevalent in bebop. Some bebop blues tunes such as "Blues for Alice" contain extra chord changes. Others, such as "Now's the Time," "Straight No Chaser," and "Tenor Madness," follow the more conventional form used below.

BLUES IN B♭

TRACK 64

Rhythm Changes

Many bebop tunes such as "Oleo" and "Moose the Mooche" are based on the chord changes of the Gershwin classic "I Got Rhythm." These tunes follow a 32-measure AABA form. The A sections make use of an 8-measure tonic-based progression. For the bridge, the song moves up a major 3rd and, using the cycle of fifths, works its way back to the tonic.

RHYTHM CHANGES IN B♭

TRACK 65

POST BOP

The mid 1950s ushered in a harder-driving style of improvisation. Guitarists such as Pat Martino, George Benson, and Grant Green expanded their palette of sounds through the use of modalism.

Bossa Nova

"Blue Bossa," "Little Sunflower," and "Song for My Father" are just a few bossa novas that were popularized in the Post Bop era.

SONG FOR MY FATHER

TRACK 66

By Horace Silver
© 1964, 1966, 1969, 1987 by Ecaroh Music, Inc.
Copyright Renewed 1992

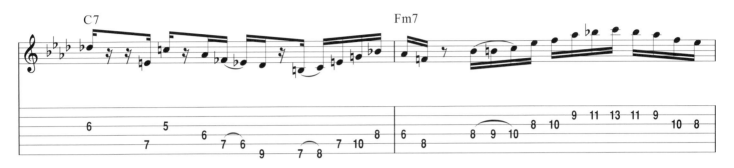

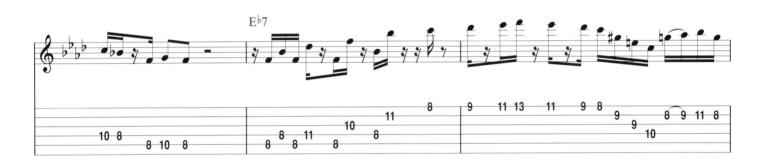

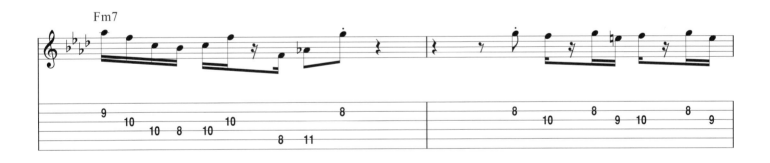

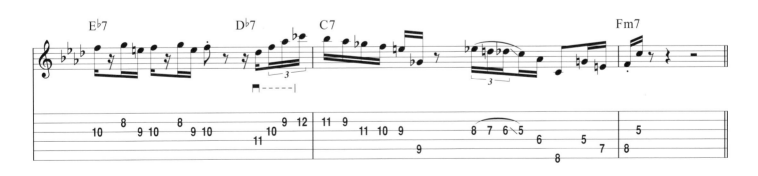

Minor Blues

"Chitlins Con Carne," "One for Daddy-O," "Equinox," and "Mr. P.C." are all common minor blues that originated in the Post Bop era.

MR. P.C.

TRACK 67

By John Coltrane
Copyright © 1977 JOWCOL MUSIC

Dominant Blues

Some of the most well-known dominant blues include "Freddie Freeloader," "Blues in the Closet," "Turnaround," and "Bessie's Blues."

BLUES IN D

TRACK 68

etc.

Funk Jazz

Funk jazz, or "soul jazz," is a subgenre of the Post Bop era that emphasizes R&B rhythms and blues-inflected improvisations. Guitarists were often found paired with organists. A few popular songs include "Mercy, Mercy, Mercy," "Sidewinder," and "Road Song."

ROAD SONG

TRACK 69

By John L. (Wes) Montgomery
Copyright © 1968 (Renewed) by TAGGIE MUSIC CO., a division of Gopam Enterprises, Inc.

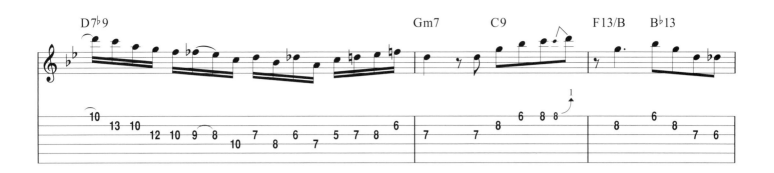

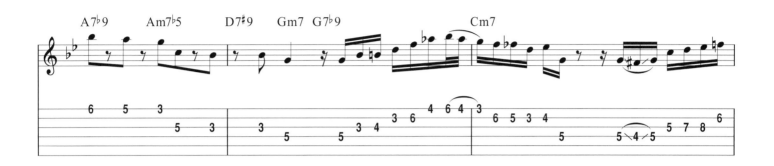

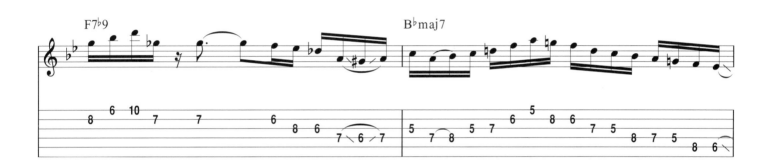

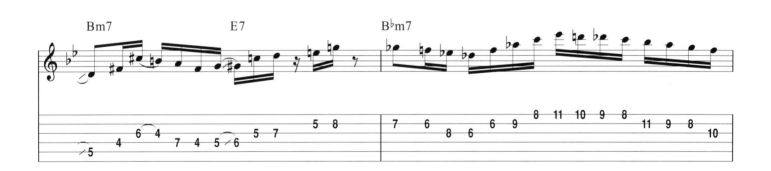

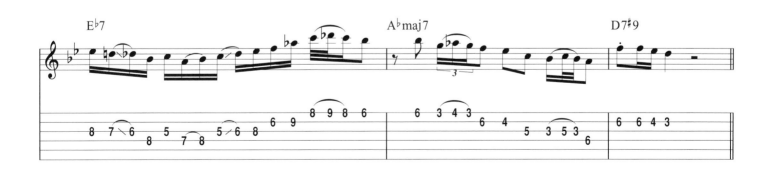

SOLO JAZZ GUITAR

Playing solo guitar means just that: you're the whole band. You provide the harmony, melody, and rhythm simultaneously—so instead of playing "rhythm" or "lead," you play the whole song. The learning curve is high, but so is the reward of being a one-man band. The following pages present a crash course on how to create solo guitar arrangements.

Generally speaking, solo guitar entails playing the melody with chords—a *chord melody*, as it is often called. The melody is the highest note in the chord, and the tones underneath generate the harmony:

AMAZING GRACE

TRACK 70

Each and every note in a song's melody is not always harmonized. Single notes, and sometimes octaves, are used to play melody notes that occur between full chords:

GREENSLEEVES

TRACK 71

The right-hand technique used for solo playing varies from player to player, so pick-style, fingerstyle, or a hybrid style using your pick and fingers together are all fine. Whatever option you choose, however, make sure that you pluck the notes of the chord evenly. One exception: play the top note in each chord slightly louder, in order to accentuate the melody. One thing to focus on with your left hand is to try to sustain the notes in the chords as long as possible. In other words, if you play a single note between two chords, maintain pressure on the strings from the first chord as you sound the next melody note.

CHORD VOICINGS

Since the building blocks for these arrangements are chords, you'll need to know a lot of voicings. At the same time, you'll need to take note of which pitch is located at the top of these voicings. That's a lot of memorization work, but you can make things easier if you look at how each chord is derived from another. For example, a major seventh chord becomes a dominant seventh by lowering one note, and a dominant seventh becomes a minor seventh by lowering one note. Below are the most common seventh chord voicings, using G as the root. Notice that all of the chords are the four-note, adjacent-string type. For most players, these voicings are best since they don't sound too bulky, and they don't require uncomfortable stretches.

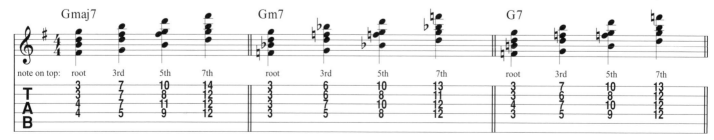

Take your time and learn as many inversions of as many chords as possible. Go back and review the chords introduced earlier in the book, and also search out additional chord voicings either on your own or with the aid of a chord encyclopedia. In all cases, memorize the interval of the top pitch.

HOW TO BUILD CHORD-MELODY ARRANGEMENTS

Once you know the chords and understand the basic concepts, you're ready to learn how to put together a chord-melody. Most arrangements begin with a lead sheet—a sketch of a song that includes the melody, lyrics (if any), and chord symbols. For starters, you can create a chord-melody arrangement from any lead sheet by simply playing voicings of the chords that contain the appropriate melody note on top, like in the example below.

SAINT JAMES INFIRMARY
TRACK 72

Notice that all of the chords in the excerpt above are plain seventh chord voicings, respective to the lead sheet, and that all of the chords contain the song's melody as their top note. Also note that the melody shown in the lead sheet has been raised an octave in order to make the tune easier to harmonize. That's the first way to do it—block chords that directly follow the chords and melody from the lead sheet. The idea isn't too difficult to grasp; you just need to know lots of voicings.

Treatment of Non-Chord, Diatonic Tones

In most cases, a song's melody will contain non-chord tones, or notes that are not within the chord given as the harmony. For example, if your melody is three notes—G, A, B—and the chord is Gmaj7, what would you do with the A note, since this note is not one of the four notes in a Gmaj7 chord? Well, here are three things to consider.

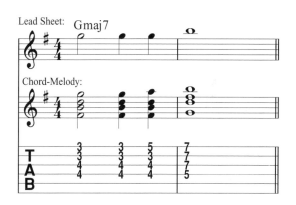

First, there's the *added note* concept. This means that if you're looking for a Gmaj7 chord with an A in the melody, you can simply find a Gmaj7 chord voicing and add the note A on top, as in the example to the right.

The "added note" concept is simple, but effective. A good way to work on this is to choose a scale, say G major, and harmonize every note using the "add-on" technique.

HARMONIZED MAJOR SCALE (ADDED NOTE CONCEPT)

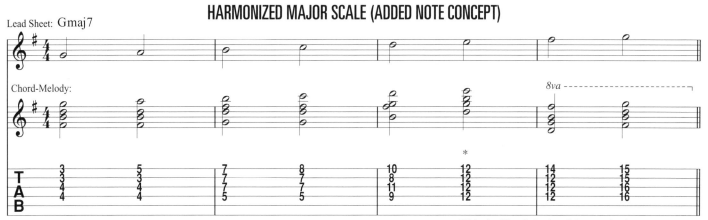

*This chord is a derivative of the next chord.

Secondly, it's common to harmonize the 2nd, 4th, and 6th degrees (the non-chord tones) of a scale by using the *ii7 chord*. In other words, instead of playing a Gmaj7 chord with an added A note on top, you can play an Am7 chord with an A on top. The following examples show how this concept plays out for major, minor, and Mixolydian scales.

HARMONIZED MAJOR SCALE (iim7 chord concept)

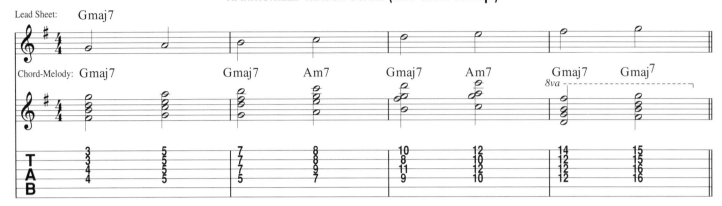

HARMONIZED MINOR SCALE (iim7 chord concept)

* G Dorian

HARMONIZED MIXOLYDIAN MODE (iim7 chord concept)

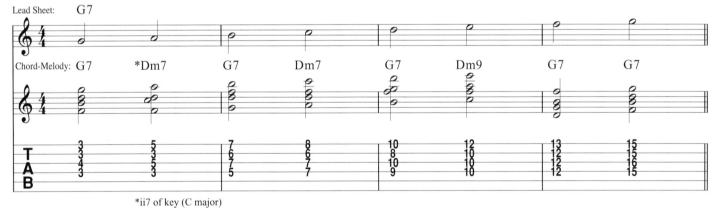

*ii7 of key (C major)

You can also use *dyads* to harmonize non-chord tones. Any interval is possible, but 3rds, 4ths, and 6ths within the key are the most common. This option—as well as using octaves and single notes—comes in handy for harmonizing faster phrases that use eighth notes or sixteenth notes.

MY ROMANCE

TRACK 73

Words by Lorenz Hart   Music by Richard Rodgers
Copyright © 1935 by Williamson Music and Lorenz Hart Publishing Co. in the United States
Copyright Renewed
All Rights Administered by Williamson Music

Treatment of Non-Chord, Chromatic Tones

To harmonize chromatic notes, you'll need to consider a few other concepts. Typically, guitarists favor the use of diminished seventh chords when harmonizing chromatic melody notes. They sound great, they come in a variety of accessible fingerings, and they're easy to use, as the example below demonstrates.

ii-V LICK USING DIMINISHED SEVENTH CHORDS

TRACK 74

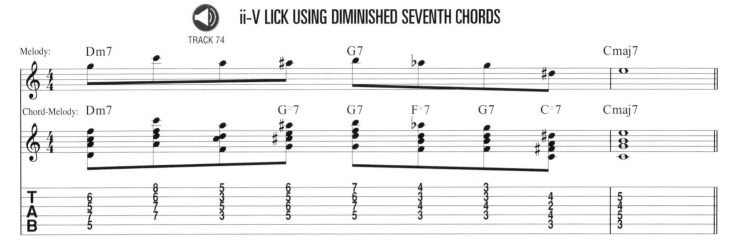

Another common approach is to move a chord up a half step. As long as the chromatic note appears briefly, this will provide a smooth transition.

LICK USING HALF STEPS

TRACK 75

Single notes, octaves, dyads, and the "add on" technique also work well for harmonizing non-chord, chromatic tones.

EXTENDED CHORDS, TRITONE SUBSTITUTION & PASSING CHORDS

Some of the chordal technique discussed earlier in the book can also be applied to chord-melody playing.

EXAMPLE USING PASSING CHORDS

TRACK 76

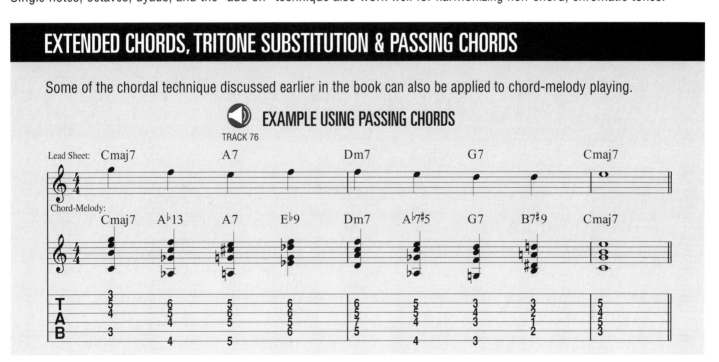

REHARMONIZATION TECHNIQUES

An important step toward being able to create an interesting chord-melody arrangement is understanding how to reharmonize a song's melody—to substitute new chords for the ones given in the original lead sheet. There are many ways to modify the chords of a song to find new harmonies. Following is an explanation of the most typical reharmonization approaches.

Diatonic Substitution

Diatonic substitutions take place when chords in a harmonized scale are used to substitute for each other. The concept takes advantage of "like qualities" and is commonly employed in three variations:

1. Substitute a ii chord for a IV chord, or vice versa. For example, in the key of C, a Dm7 may replace an Fmaj7, and an Fmaj7 may replace a Dm7.

2. Substitute a V chord for a vii°7 chord, or vice versa. For example, in the key of C, a G7 may replace a Bm7♭5, and a Bm7♭5 may replace a G7.

3. I, iii, and vi chords are all interchangeable. For example, in the key of C, Cmaj7, Em7, and Am7 can be substituted for one another.

The following example applies all three diatonic substitution techniques.

LOOK FOR THE SILVER LINING
TRACK 77

Minor Third Substitution

The ii chord and/or V chord in a ii–V–I progression can be substituted with the same chord a minor 3rd higher.

TRACK 78

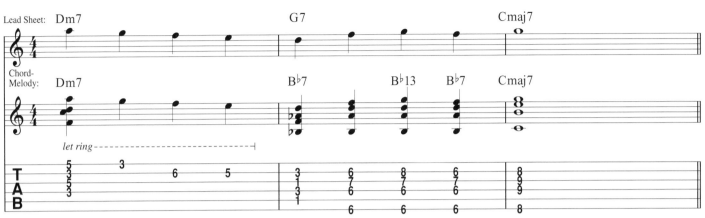

Backcycling

Backcycling (a.k.a. "cycle of fourths" substitution) occurs when a song's written chord is preceded by a chord a 4th below. In most instances, the written chord(s) is delayed while you work your way back through the cycle of fourths.

The next example demonstrates backcycling, as well as a few other reharmonization techniques we've discussed.

GIVE MY REGARDS TO BROADWAY

TRACK 79

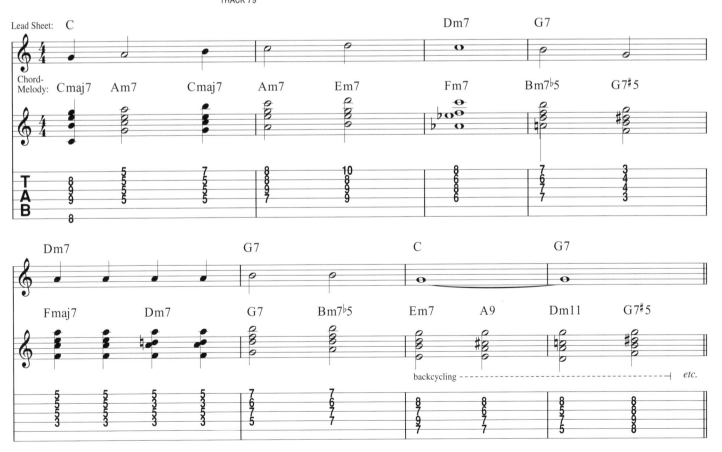

Other Suggestions

The beautiful thing about chord-melody is that there are so many ways to approach it. Here are a few other concepts to consider. First, pay attention to *voice leading*—the movement of individual notes from one chord to another. Ideally, a four-note chord should resolve to a four-note chord, and the distance each interval has to travel from one chord to the next should be minimal. Secondly, try mixing in a few improvised single-note phrases. In ballads and other slow-tempo tunes where the melody is built from whole notes and half notes, this technique of filling in the gaps works great. Thirdly, bear in mind that you can raise or lower the 5th degree in a major or minor chord, and you can raise or lower the 5th and 9th degrees in a dominant chord. And lastly, don't carve your arrangements in stone. Each time you play through a song, try something new.

Following is a sample chord-melody phrase that uses many of the concepts introduced in this section.

TRACK 80

THE CHRISTMAS SONG
(Chestnuts Roasting on an Open Fire)

Music and Lyric by Mel Torme and Robert Wells
© 1946 (Renewed) EDWIN H. MORRIS & COMPANY, A Division of MPL Communications, Inc.

THE MELODY

Jazz guitarists generally approach the melody, or "head," of a song in one of four ways:

1. Single notes
2. Octaves
3. Chord-melody
4. Combination of options 1-3

When playing the head with single notes, as in the example below, it is common to embellish the written melody by adding simple fills and ornaments.

I REMEMBER YOU

TRACK 81

from the Paramount Picture THE FLEET'S IN
Words by Johnny Mercer   Music by Victor Schertzinger
Copyright © 1942 (Renewed 1969) by Paramount Music Corporation

The next example employs octaves. You can either pluck the notes with your thumb, pick, or combination of pick and fingers. Try all three options, and use what sounds best to you.

INDIANA

TRACK 82

Now try playing the first eight measures of "Misty." Notice that single notes, octaves, and chord-melody are all used.

MISTY

TRACK 83

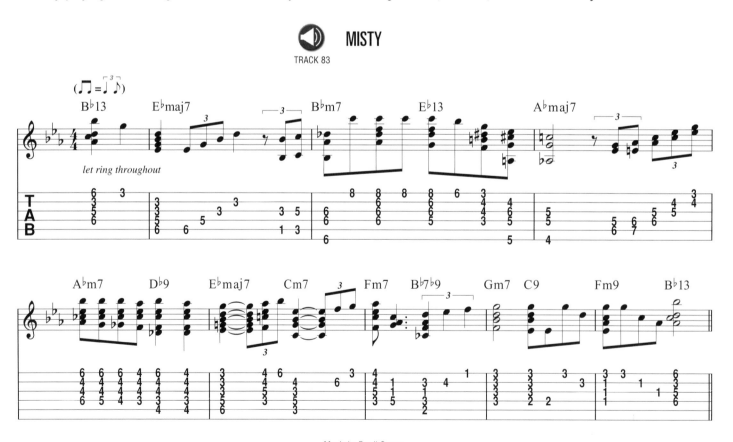

Music by Erroll Garner

INTROS & ENDINGS

There are numerous ways to begin and end a jazz song. Most fake books and lead sheets usually do not include these specific elements; instead, jazz musicians either compose something on the spot or rely on a few stock phrases that most band members are likely to be familiar with.

INTROS

Intros are used to establish the key and set the tempo. They can also suggest a mood and add interest to an arrangement. One of the most common ways to set up the top of a tune is to play the song's "last eight" measures. Here are some additional tried-and-true intros.

The next two intros work well leading into a blues progression.

TURNAROUND TO THE I7

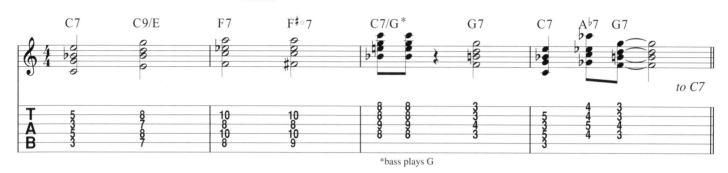

*bass plays G

DESCENDING BASS LINE TO THE I7

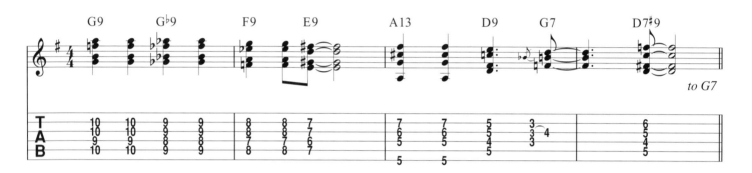

to G7

Here are two common bossa nova intros.

I—IV BOSSA VAMP

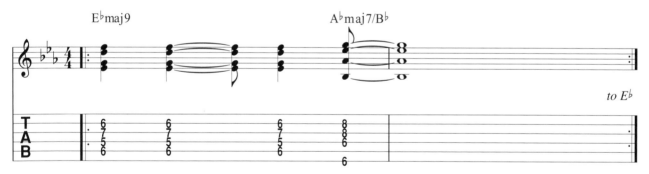

to E♭

I—♭VII BOSSA VAMP

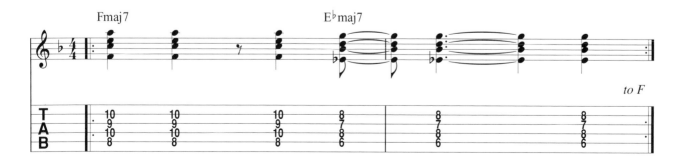

to F

The following intros work well leading intro songs in minor keys.

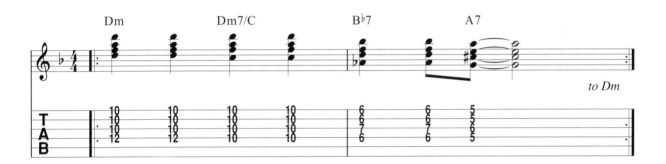

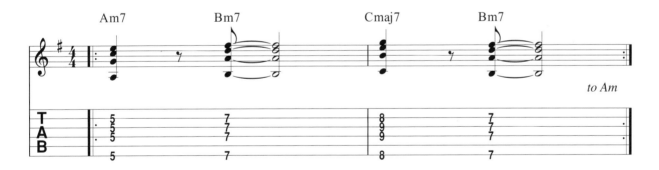

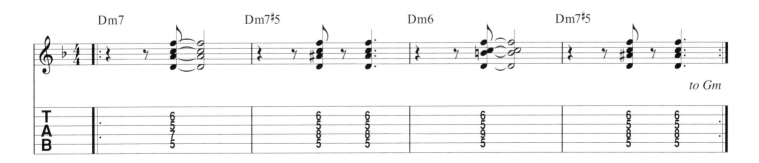

ENDINGS

A good ending should bring the song to an obvious finish. The most common ending is the "triple tag," which extends the song's form by repeating the last four measures three times.

Following are some timeless devices that will ensure you "put the song to bed" safely.

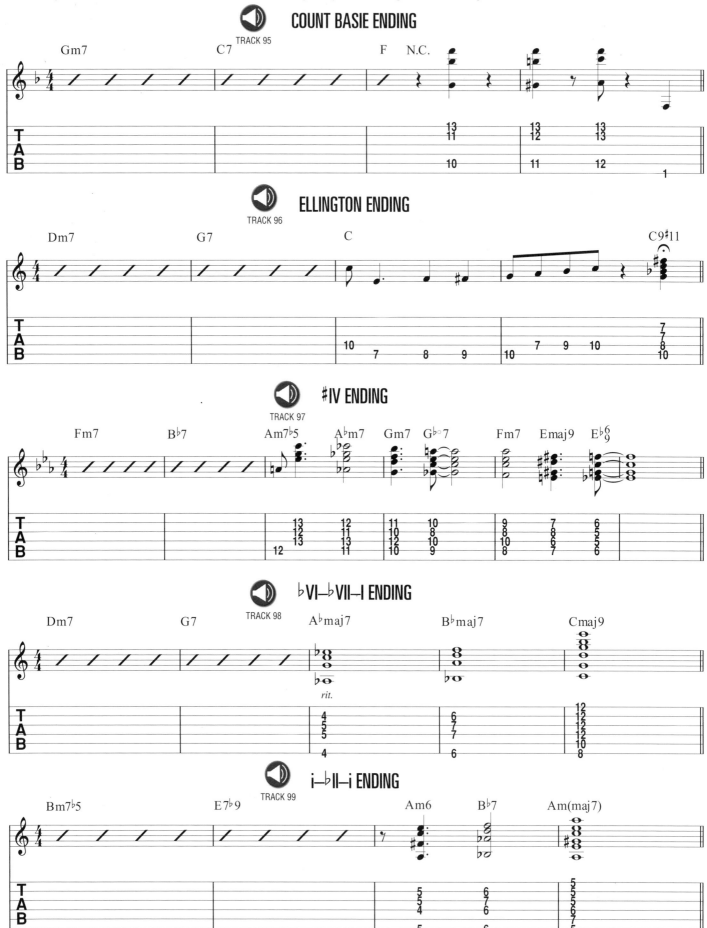